A. J. Liebling (1904–1963) joined the staff of *The New Yorker* in 1935, where his 'Wayward Press' columns became a model of fine journalistic writing. His many books include *The Telephone Booth Indian*, *The Road Back to Paris*, *The Sweet Science: A Ringside View of Boxing*, *The Earl of Louisiana*, *Normandy Revisited* and *Liebling at Home*.

A. J. LIEBLING

BETWEEN MEALS

An Appetite for Paris

With an introduction by James Salter

CARDÍNAL

A CARDINAL BOOK

First published in the USA by North Point Press 1986

First published in Great Britain by Sphere Books Ltd in Cardinal 1990

Copyright © A. J. Liebling 1959, 1962, 1981, 1986

Introduction copyright © James Salter 1986

Reproduced, printed and bound in Great Britain by
The Guernsey Press Co. Ltd, Guernsey, Channel Islands.

ISBN 0 7474 0557 3

Sphere Books Ltd
A Division of
Macdonald & Co. (Publishers) Ltd
27 Wrights Lane, London W8 5TZ
A member of Maxwell Pergamon Publishing Corporation plc

TO YVES MIRANDE

Contents

Introduction
by James Salter

A. J. LIEBLING belonged
to the generation, now gone, that lived through
both World Wars and, further, to that fabled
splinter of it that knew Paris in what seems to us
its most glorious days. He was a journalist all his
life, beginning as a provincial reporter, then moving to New York, working for several papers there,
and finally becoming a writer for *The New Yorker*.
He possessed from the first and gradually perfected
a very idiomatic style, one of precision, ease, and
richness of detail. It won him the devotion of readers as well as friends. The voice becomes unmistakable, that of a large, unkempt man with a gift as
exact as Cyril Connolly's, rummaging around in a
huge bin of what might be called demi-classical
references: literary, gastronomic, sporting, historic.

Journalists cannot expect their work to last.
Even Dreiser's or Hemingway's articles are of little
interest to us. Though the standards for prose at
The New Yorker were and are unusually high, there
is only so much room in the stacks to be given to
things of passing concern, and magazine pieces
are not the path to being remembered.

Autobiography, though, is another matter, as is
memoir and in this book, most of which appeared
originally as a series of four articles, we have a
mixture of both, done with an elegance and wit
that make one feel it may endure. It is Liebling's
last book, published just before the end, although
the writing in it was spread over twenty years and
takes in more than fifty, from his earliest visits to
Paris as a child—he was born in 1904—to almost
his final trip a few months before his death in
1963, when, tired, ill, unable to write, he made a
late summer journey to France, probably knowing
he would not see it again.

He had remarkable talent although he may not
have made the best use of it. As many other reporters have done, he dreamed of being a novelist
or short story writer with newspapers only a way
station on the road to greatness, but though he had
a novelist's eye he was for some reason never able
to become one. He wrote occasional short stories
during his career and made at least one attempt to
write a novel but gave it up. He finally settled for
what he had begun as, a journalist, loving and hat-
ing it at the same time, its privileges, irregular
hours, allure. "The taint was on me," he wrote of
himself, and driven by habit and need of money he

continued for years never out of debt to the magazine for which he wrote prodigiously. He knew his abilities—he was fond of saying that he could write better than anyone who could write faster, and faster than anyone who could write better, and he could sit down in his cluttered office and in an afternoon or evening turn out four or five thousand impeccable words without getting winded. It was hard work but he knew how to do it. He also knew the melancholy of having recognition come late. His personal life was not happy. He was married three times. His first wife was mentally ill and unfaithful. She was a good looking, uneducated Irish girl whom he had met when she was working in a movie box office in Providence. His parents disapproved of the marriage. He was Jewish and she was not; she was of a lower class. After fifteen years and long separation during which she was in and out of institutions they were divorced, although he remained loyal to her and continued to send her money all his life. His second wife was beautiful and extravagant, a divorcée with a teen-age daughter. She left him unexpectedly. His third and last wife was the writer Jean Stafford, who had once been married to Robert Lowell.

Physically, Liebling was not attractive yet women liked him. Bald, overweight, and gluttonous was how he described himself. He ate and drank to excess. He was shy and given to long silences. He wore glasses. His feet were flat and it was painful for him to walk, especially in later life when he had gotten so large that it was impossible, a fellow writer said, to walk beside him on the sidewalk. He also had gout. Despite this women were often fond of him, even pretty women. As a friend of his explained, he made them feel intelligent. This was not a tactic, it was genuine.

The son of an immigrant who did very well for himself as a furrier, Liebling had rebelled against his bourgeois upbringing. He saw his father's New York world as soulless and gross and while remaining an affectionate son he nevertheless stubbornly went his own way, choosing things that were contrary to what might be expected. German by background, he rejected Germany for France. In school his companions were athletes, some less than admirable, and the girls he fell in love with were gentile. His pull was towards the disreputable elements of society, the seamy part of life, men who lived by their wits, and he wrote about petty crooks, politicians, and phonies. It was the Dickensian layer of the city he was drawn to. His sympathies were with the little man, the underdog; he liked people who led unconventional lives. He was at ease with them and they with him, a big, rumpled figure with a homely face and his navel showing through an unbuttoned shirt. He wrote especially well of boxing, the thrilling, soiled world of fighters, their managers and trainers. He had boxed a little himself, not particularly well, and retained a great interest in it.

When he was twenty-two his father, who had never known much leisure himself until late in life, generously gave him the gift of a year of study at the Sorbonne and it is that year that is the emotional center of this book. He attended very few classes but learned things that stood him in good stead for the rest of his life.

The year was 1926–27 and the Paris he discovered is like Cafavy's Alexandria, William Kennedy's Albany, or Bellow's Chicago—a city seen mainly from the underside with occasional glimpses into upper realms. The book is a kind of guide to a legendary Paris, parts of which no longer exist. Liebling was collecting, like the bits of string and shiny metal the magpie brings back to its nest, the discarded things that carry emotional power, fragments of a fabulous and disappearing city, the same city that Hemingway and Gertrude Stein fell in love with, a city in the 1920s exhausted by the effort of four years of war with huge casualties, and weary despite the final triumph. The face was still ravishing but the tone of the skin had lost its freshness and there were faint lines in the brow and around the mouth.

There are no famous names strewn here. It was all lived and written beyond the illumination of art and fashion, but here is Paris in the days when there were brothels that were visited by princes— the most famous of them was on the rue Chabanais and there are the photographs by Brassai of others. The aristocracy of Russia, which had fled revolution and civil war, was driving taxicabs and working in nightclubs, and in a few minutes Lindberg was to arrive.

Waverly Root, who was a food writer and Liebling's friend and whose book *The Food of France* is a kind of shadowy companion to Liebling's, was a young newspaperman in Paris at the time. Lindbergh had landed at Le Bourget and in his memoirs Root tells of an unbelievable crowd swarming towards the plane and someone climbing up to grab the leather helmet from Lindbergh's head and waving it in the air. The mob, mistaking him for the hero, bore him off on its shoulders. There were South American playboys living in Paris who boasted they had never seen it in daylight—they rose in the evenings and went to bed before dawn. It was a city of luxury and light and of course of their extreme opposites, drabness and poverty. But Paris was then and in many ways remains first among all the cities of the world. The French way of living, the French outlook on things, French literature, art, films, cuisine, not to speak of architecture, ocean liners, automobiles—these were the highest standard that existed and even now one looks back at them with admiration.

All this was there when Liebling spent his memorable year. Even so, it was only what remained of the period before 1914 when the brilliance was untarnished. As Yves Mirande wrote of it then:

. . . Paris was radiant, elegant, and refined. In the world and in the half-world, feasts followed upon feasts, wild nights upon vertiginous suppers. It was the courtesans' *grand époque*. Innocent of preoccupation with the future, they had no trace of a desire to build up an income for old age. They were gamblers, beautiful gamblers, with a certain natural distinction in their

ways and a *je ne sais quoi* of good breeding—
the bonnet thrown over the windmill, but without falling into vulgarity or coarseness. . . .

This vanishing world was left in mere traces
just as the 1920s themselves are traces now. And
of course it was cheap, beautiful and cheap in a
way one can no longer imagine. The franc was
twenty-six to the dollar and a diner at Lapèrouse
cost fifty francs. It was easy to find places in which
to live and the frankness and sexuality of the city
were dazzling, especially to Americans who had
known only the Puritanism of their own country,
its materialism, indifference to art and ignorance
of history. They came to France to breathe new air.
Many writers, Americans and others, came and
some of them wrote important books. Beckett was
just arriving in Paris where he would soon meet
James Joyce, Jean Rhys was there, Ford Maddox
Ford had established the *Transatlantic Review*,
Pound was just pulling up stakes and moving to
Rapallo, and Henry Miller was in the wings. Liebling was removed from all of this, he lived outside
it. He had never published anything and was only
twenty-two, with very particular ideas about pleasure: he liked to walk, read, he was given to com-
fort, he especially liked to eat. In a simple but
beautiful epithet he says of those days, "I was often
alone, but seldom lonely." This is a pronouncement
that Pascal would have admired.

Liebling came back to Paris many times, in
1939 as a war correspondent for *The New Yorker*

after an absence of twelve years, in 1944 when Paris was liberated, and frequently after the war, and his focus in the city shifted gradually upwards, from the 5th and 6th arrondisements to the 2nd and over towards the 16th, which is to say from the academic to the mercantile. In these later years his concern with food became even more obsessive. He proposed calling the articles upon which the book is based *Recollections of a Gourmet in France* but his editor protested that there was no way in which Liebling could so describe himself and "gourmet" was changed finally to "feeder." He was by now legendary as a glutton. However it had begun it had become an essential part of him, a consolation, a rebellion, a plume, and in the end he destroyed himself through gluttony with kidney and heart trouble and his fingers, toes, and even ears disfigured by gout. In his last years there were great depressions and manic highs. He was zooming and then plunging, the arcs becoming steeper, and at the same time he was writing almost continually. He was like a blind mill horse doomed to spend the rest of his life trudging in a circle which for him was crowds, restaurants, racetracks, the *New Yorker* offices, boxing matches. He had given up on his appearance but was living lavishly, his stepdaughter in private schools, his wife stylishly dressed. Amid all this he recollected and set down a pure vision of earlier years. Though not a novel it has a novel's grip—there is dialogue, character, description, and the unmistakable signature of a real writer: an entire book thrown away on nearly every page. The result is astonishingly fresh and deserves to stand on the same shelf as *A Moveable Feast* with which I think it may be reasonably compared.

Many things first came into my life or at least into my awareness when I read the *New Yorker* articles: de Ségonzac, vermouth cassis, Grands-Echezeaux, *brandade de morue*. Other things I already knew or had read elsewhere but Liebling confirmed them and he is someone you trust. You do not read him for information, of course, but it is inescapable and some things have not changed that much. The streets and squares of Paris are the same. There is still a Chez Benoit, no longer the unspoiled Lyonnais bistro it is true, polished up, larger, and a favorite of tourists, but the kitchen is the same. There is still Pierre's on the Place Gaillon, Drouant, and the Closerie de Lilas where Hemingway used to sit in the afternoon and watch the light change. There is still a restaurant Sorg in Strasbourg and it retains a star in the Michelin, a book Liebling held in disdain, not for any inaccuracy or lack of standards but because it is a symbol of the age of the automobile and the decline, in his view, of provincial restaurants in France. This may seem to be a contradiction but the speed and ease of car travel has meant that restaurants which once depended on a steady, discriminating clientele of business travelers now need only cater to customers who come once and are unlikely to return, at least for some time. As a result the restaurants rarely change their menus and are not pressed to satisfy unfailingly, cook seasonal specialties, or try new dishes. A kind of anonymous patronage, such as one might find in a shoeshine parlor, leads to a lower level of art. Apart from this there is always a risk that, while hotels and restaurants still exist, they are perhaps of altered attractiveness, like an old girlfriend revisited, as Liebling himself might say.

Nearly everyone I know in my generation went to Europe, either during the war or in the majority of cases soon afterwards. They were all just out of the army or just out of school, fresh, eager for the great experience which then was represented by Paris more than any place else. At that time it still prided itself as the capital of art, literature, philosophy, and a kind of glamorous corruption. To go there was a rite, an ambition, a dream. I arrived in January, 1950, almost twenty-five years after Liebling. I was coming to Europe for the first time. How imperishable that is. The strangeness of it, the newness, its shapes and smells. I remember the grey, wintry aspect of the Champs-Elysèes when I first saw it, wider than it is now, almost empty of cars. I don't remember my first meal. I had never bought a *Paris Tribune* or heard of Waverly Root. I had no idea who was buried in Père Lachaise or where Victor Hugo's fifteen or twenty places of residence in Paris were. I hadn't heard of the *Guide Michelin* and it would have been of little use to me if I had. I would have been more interested in the *Guide Rose*, a reputed guide to French brothels that was published before the war although I have never been able to find a copy of it and it remains for me one of the lost, exotic fragments.

In my pocket were notes that had been given to me by a friend who had been to Europe a number of times. He was an older man, a sophisticated New Yorker. He had written a successful play, been an escort of debutantes and elected to clubs. He had a broad, Rooseveltian charm, even to the discolored tusks, a haughty second wife and a dachshund named Freddy Barker. I can still see his green fountain pen and patrician handwriting as he made a long list of things for me on index cards. There were hotels like the Vendome, near the Ritz on the Place Vendome and much less expensive, and places like Monseigneur—go after eleven when the girls begin showing up at the bar, he wrote. Those were days, it is true, when I was living from the waist down, as Maurice Chevalier once said, but not on that scale. I had very little money, knew no one, and buttered the extra breakfast roll to save it for lunch.

Travel and tourism have changed since then and immeasurably since Liebling's time. The world has been opened up by jet aircraft and credit cards and it is difficult to remember that the Paris and France of the 1920s were almost as distant and unexploited as Australia or Nepal are today. This is not to say that they were unvisited, merely that the whole world did not tramp through. One traveled, at least from America, by boat, which is how Liebling left in 1927, sailing home from Marseilles after the year which formed his life on an old boat which, as it happened, blew up and capsized twenty years later, in Haifa, after the war. In a sense he became that old boat and although he lasted two decades longer he finally sank far from the shores he had loved.

He was a strange case. He was entirely secular with no apparent spiritual side. He found and wrote of a world of borderline people—the first article for *The New Yorker* that brought him notice was a profile of the black religious leader, Father Divine. He was a Francophile, and admired French writers, Rabelais and Céline, and across the way Dickens and Christopher Marlowe. He particularly admired a nineteenth-century chronicler of the London prize ring named Pierce Egan and quoted him as Montaigne might quote Seneca. Despite his talent he failed to carve out a lasting place for himself and lived a shifting, almost precarious life as did those who were his favorite subjects. It was as if, the eternal schoolboy, fat and disheveled, he continued to find things of greater interest than those in the curriculum and he and his more conventional classmates parted ways. He had been kicked out of Dartmouth and he was never reclaimed.

I met him once, about 1960, in the offices of *The New Yorker*. It was in the evening and the place was empty. He was wearing a dark suit with the rosette of the Legion of Honor in his lapel. He seemed shy and walked with difficulty, as if in pain, as if his feet were too dainty for the rest of the architecture. His glasses were round and steel-rimmed. His bald head seemed a little battered, like an old pie plate. I don't remember anything he said. It was very brief. Still, I remember it vividly because I admired him so. I had read nearly everything he had written and in the 1950s as his work became more autobiographical and he included greater fragments of his life in it I formed an estimable picture of the author which was not altered when I met him in the flesh. I had the mistaken idea that he had been a good boxer in college which made me respect the extra weight he was now carrying as one might respect the stiffness of a limb on a veteran soldier.

He died three years later. His last words were spoken in an ambulance as he was being driven between hospitals. They could not be made out, but they were in French. He is buried in Springs, at the eastern end of Long Island where for some years he had a house. His luminous account lives on. It possesses many of the qualities he ascribed to his favorite wines. It stimulates the senses, assists in clarity of view, and provides a feeling of approval towards life such as one gets in fine museums or walking along handsome streets.

BETWEEN
MEALS

I

A Good Appetite

The Proust *madeleine* phenomenon is now as firmly established in folklore as Newton's apple or Watt's steam kettle. The man ate a tea biscuit, the taste evoked memories, he wrote a book. This is capable of expression by the formula TMB, for Taste > Memory > Book. Some time ago, when I began to read a book called *The Food of France,* by Waverley Root, I had an inverse experience: BMT, for Book > Memory > Taste. Happily, the tastes that *The Food of France* re-created for me—small birds, stewed rabbit, stuffed tripe, Côte Rôtie, and Tavel—were more robust than that of the *madeleine,* which Larousse defines as "a light cake made with sugar, flour, lemon juice, brandy, and eggs." (The quantity of brandy in a *madeleine* would not furnish a gnat with an alcohol rub.) In the light of what Proust wrote with so mild a stimulus, it is the world's loss that he did not have a heartier appetite. On a dozen Gardiners Island oysters, a bowl of clam chowder, a peck of steamers, some bay scallops, three sautéed soft-shelled crabs, a few ears of fresh-picked corn, a thin swordfish steak of generous area, a pair of lobsters, and a Long Island duck, he might have written a masterpiece.

The primary requisite for writing well about food is a good appetite. Without this, it is impossible to accumulate, within the allotted span, enough experience of eating to have anything worth setting down. Each day brings only two opportunities for field work, and they are not to be wasted minimizing the intake of cholesterol. They are indispensable, like a prizefighter's hours on the road. (I have read that the late French professional gourmand Maurice Curnonsky ate but one meal a day—dinner. But that was late in his life, and I have always suspected his attainments anyway; so many mediocre witticisms are attributed to him that he could not have had much time for eating.) A good appetite gives an eater room to turn around in. For example, a nonprofessional eater I know went to the Restaurant Pierre, in the Place Gaillon, a couple of years ago, his mind set on a sensibly light meal: a dozen, or possibly eighteen, oysters, and a thick chunk of steak topped with beef marrow, which M. Pierre calls a *Délice de la Villette*—the equivalent of a "Stockyards' Delight." But as he arrived, he heard M. Pierre say to his headwaiter, "Here comes Monsieur L. Those two portions of *cassoulet* that are

4

left—put them aside for him." A *cassoulet* is a substantial dish, of a complexity precluding its discussion here. (Mr. Root devotes three pages to the great controversy over what it should contain.) M. Pierre is the most amiable of restaurateurs, who prides himself on knowing in advance what his friends will like. A client of limited appetite would be obliged either to forgo his steak or to hurt M. Pierre's feelings. Monsieur L., however, was in no difficulty. He ate the two *cassoulets,* as was his normal practice; if he had consumed only one, his host would have feared that it wasn't up to standard. He then enjoyed his steak. The oysters offered no problem, since they present no bulk.

In the heroic age before the First World War, there were men and women who ate, in addition to a whacking lunch and a glorious dinner, a voluminous *souper* after the theater or the other amusements of the evening. I have known some of the survivors, octogenarians of unblemished appetite and unfailing good humor—spry, wry, and free of the ulcers that come from worrying about a balanced diet—but they have had no emulators in France since the doctors there discovered the existence of the human liver. From that time on, French life has been built to an increasing extent around that organ, and a niggling caution has replaced the old recklessness; the liver was the seat of the Maginot mentality. One of the last of the great around-the-clock gastronomes of France was Yves Mirande, a small, merry author of farces and musical-comedy books.

In 1955, Mirande celebrated his eightieth birthday
with a speech before the curtain of the Théâtre
Antoine, in the management of which he was
associated with Mme. B., a protégée of his, forty
years younger than himself. But the theater was
only half of his life. In addition, M. Mirande was
an unofficial director of a restaurant on the Rue
Saint-Augustin, which he had founded for another
protégée, also forty years younger than himself;
this was Mme. G., a Gasconne and a magnificent
cook. In the restaurant on the Rue Saint-Augustin,
M. Mirande would dazzle his juniors, French and
American, by dispatching a lunch of raw Bayonne
ham and fresh figs, a hot sausage in crust, spindles
of filleted pike in a rich rose *sauce Nantua*, a leg
of lamb larded with anchovies, artichokes on a
pedestal of foie gras, and four or five kinds of
cheese, with a good bottle of Bordeaux and one of
champagne, after which he would call for the
Armagnac and remind Madame to have ready for
dinner the larks and ortolans she had promised
him, with a few *langoustes* and a turbot—and, of
course, a fine *civet* made from the *marcassin*, or
young wild boar, that the lover of the leading
lady in his current production had sent up from
his estate in the Sologne. "And while I think of it,"
I once heard him say, "we haven't had any woodcock for days, or truffles baked in the ashes, and
the cellar is becoming a disgrace—no more '34s
and hardly any '37s. Last week, I had to offer my
publisher a bottle that was far too good for him,
simply because there was nothing between the
insulting and the superlative."

M. Mirande had to his credit a hundred produced plays, including a number of great Paris hits, but he had just written his first book for print, so he said "my publisher" in a special mock-impressive tone. "An informal sketch for my definitive autobiography," he would say of this production. The informal sketch, which I cherish, begins with the most important decision in Mirande's life. He was almost seventeen and living in the small Breton port of Lannion—his offstage family name was Le Querrec—when his father, a retired naval officer, said to him, "It is time to decide your future career. Which will it be, the Navy or the Church?" No other choice was conceivable in Lannion. At dawn, Yves ran away to Paris.

There, he had read a thousand times, all the famous wits and cocottes frequented the tables in front of the Café Napolitain, on the Boulevard des Capucines. He presented himself at the café at nine the next morning—late in the day for Lannion—and found that the place had not yet opened. Soon he became a newspaperman. It was a newspaper era as cynically animated as the corresponding period of the Bennett-Pulitzer-Hearst competition in New York, and in his second or third job he worked for a press lord who was as notional and niggardly as most press lords are; the publisher insisted that his reporters be well turned out, but did not pay them salaries that permitted cab fares when it rained. Mirande lived near the fashionable Montmartre cemetery and solved his rainy-day pants-crease problem by crashing funeral parties as they broke up and riding, gratis, in the carriages returning to the center of town. Early in his career, he became personal secretary to Clemenceau and then to Briand, but the gay theater attracted him more than politics, and he made the second great decision of his life after one of his political patrons had caused him to be appointed *sous-préfet* in a provincial city. A *sous-préfet* is the administrator of one of the districts into which each of the ninety *départements* of France is divided, and a young *sous-préfet* is often headed for a precocious rise to high positions of state. Mirande, attired in the magnificent uniform that was then de rigueur, went to his "capital," spent one night there, and then ran off to Paris again to direct a one-act farce. Nevertheless, his connections with the serious world remained cordial. In the restaurant on the Rue Saint-Augustin, he introduced me to Colette, by that time a national glory of letters.

The regimen fabricated by Mirande's culinary protégée, Mme. G., maintained him *en pleine forme*. When I first met him, in the restaurant, during the summer of the Liberation, he was a sprightly sixty-nine. In the spring of 1955, when we renewed a friendship that had begun in admiration of each other's appetite, he was as good as ever. On the occasion of our reunion, we began with a *truite au bleu*—a live trout simply done to death in hot water, like a Roman emperor in his bath. It was served up doused with enough melted butter to thrombose a regiment of Paul Dudley Whites, and accompanied, as was right, by an Alsatian wine—a Lacrimae Sanctae Odiliae, which once contributed slightly to my education. Long ago, when I was very young, I took out a woman in Strasbourg and, wishing to impress her with my knowledge of local customs, ordered a bottle of Ste. Odile. I was making the same mistake as if I had taken out a girl in Boston and offered her baked beans. "How quaint!" the woman in Strasbourg said. "I haven't drunk that for years." She excused herself to go to the telephone, and never came back.

After the trout, Mirande and I had two meat courses, since we could not decide in advance which we preferred. We had a magnificent *daube provençale*, because we were faithful to *la cuisine bourgeoise*, and then *pintadous*—young guinea hens, simply and tenderly roasted—with the first asparagus of the year, to show our fidelity to *la cuisine classique*. We had clarets with both courses —a Pétrus with the *daube*, a Cheval Blanc with the guineas. Mirande said that his doctor had discounseled Burgundies. It was the first time in our acquaintance that I had heard him admit he had a doctor, but I was reassured when he drank a bottle and a half of Krug after luncheon. We had three bottles between us—one to our loves, one to our countries, and one for symmetry, the last being on the house.

Mirande was a small, alert man with the face of a Celtic terrier—salient eyebrows and an up-turned nose. He looked like an intelligent Lloyd George. That summer, in association with Mme. B., his theatrical protégée, he planned to produce

a new play of Sartre's. His mind kept young by the
theater of Mme. B., his metabolism protected by
the restaurant of Mme. G., Mirande seemed forti-
fied against all eventualities for at least another
twenty years. Then, perhaps, he would have to
recruit new protégées. The Sunday following our
reunion, I encountered him at Longchamp, a race-
course where the restaurant does not face the
horses, and diners can keep first things first. There
he sat, radiant, surrounded by celebrities and
champagne buckets, sending out a relay team of
commissionaires to bet for him on the successive
tips that the proprietors of stables were ravished
to furnish him between races. He was the em-
bodiment of a happy man. (I myself had a nice
thing at 27-1.)

The first alteration in Mirande's fortunes affected me so directly that I did not at once sense
its gravity for him. Six weeks later, I was again in
Paris. (That year, I was shuttling frequently between there and London.) I was alone on the
evening I arrived, and looked forward to a pleasant
dinner at Mme. G.'s, which was within two hundred metres of the hotel, in the Square Louvois,
where I always stop. Madame's was more than a
place to eat, although one ate superbly there.
Arriving, I would have a bit of talk with the proprietress, then with the waitresses—Germaine and
Lucienne—who had composed the original staff.
Waiters had been added as the house prospered,
but they were of less marked personality. Madame
was a bosomy woman—voluble, tawny, with a
big nose and lank black hair—who made one

think of a Saracen. (The Saracens reached Gascony in the eighth century.) Her conversation was a chronicle of letters and the theater—as good as a subscription to *Figaro Littéraire*, but more advanced. It was somewhere between the avantgarde and the main body, but within hailing distance of both and enriched with the names of the great people who had been in recently—M. Cocteau, Gene Kelly, la Comtesse de Vogüé. It was always well to give an appearance of listening, lest she someday fail to save for you the last order of larks *en brochette* and bestow them on a more attentive customer. With Germaine and Lucienne, whom I had known when we were all younger, in 1939, the year of the *drôle de guerre*, flirtation was now perfunctory, but the *carte du jour* was still the serious topic—for example, how the fat Belgian industrialist from Tournai had reacted to the *caille vendangeuse*, or quail potted with fresh grapes. "You know the man," Germaine would say. "If it isn't dazzling, he takes only two portions. But when he has three, then you can say to yourself . . ." She and Lucienne looked alike—compact little women, with high foreheads and cheekbones and solid, muscular legs, who walked like *chasseurs à pied*, a hundred and thirty steps to the minute. In 1939, and again in 1944, Germaine had been a brunette and Lucienne a blonde, but in 1955 Germaine had become a blonde, too, and I found it hard to tell them apart.

Among my fellow customers at Mme. G.'s I was always likely to see some friend out of the past. It is a risk to make an engagement for an entire evening with somebody you haven't seen for years. This is particularly true in France now. The almost embarrassingly pro-American acquaintance of the Liberation may be by now a Communist Party-line hack; the idealistic young Resistance journalist may have become an editorial writer for the reactionary newspaper of a textile magnate. The Vichy apologist you met in Washington in 1941, who called de Gaulle a traitor and the creation of the British Intelligence Service, may now tell you that the General is the best thing ever, while the fellow you knew as a de Gaulle aide in London may now compare him to Sulla destroying the Roman Republic. As for the women, who is to say which of them has resisted the years? But in a good restaurant that all have frequented, you are likely to meet any of them again, for good restaurants are not so many nowadays that a Frenchman will permanently desert one—unless, of course, he is broke, and in that case it would depress you to learn of his misfortunes. If you happen to encounter your old friends when they are already established at their tables, you have the opportunity to greet them cordially and to size them up. If you still like them, you can make a further engagement.

On the ghastly evening I speak of—a beautiful one in June—I perceived no change in the undistinguished exterior of Mme. G.'s restaurant. The name—something like Prospéria—was the same, and since the plate-glass windows were backed with scrim, it was impossible to see inside. Nor, indeed, did I notice any difference when I first entered. The bar, the tables, the banquettes covered with leatherette, the simple décor of mirrors and pink marble slabs were the same. The premises had been a business employees' bar-and-café before Mme. G., succeeding a long string of obscure proprietors, made it illustrious. She had changed the fare and the clientele but not the cadre. There are hundreds of identical fronts and interiors in Paris, turned out by some mass producer in the late twenties. I might have been warned by the fact that the room was empty, but it was only eight o'clock and still light outdoors. I had come unusually early because I was so hungry. A man whom I did not recognize came to meet me, rubbing his hands and hailing me as an old acquaintance. I thought he might be a waiter who had served me. (The waiters, as I have said, were not the marked personalities of the place.) He had me at a table before I sensed the trap.

"Madame goes well?" I asked politely.

"No, Madame is lightly ill," he said, with what I now realize was a guilty air.

He presented me with a *carte du jour* written in the familiar purple ink on the familiar wide sheet of paper with the name and telephone number of the restaurant at the top. The content of the menu, however, had become Italianized, the spelling had deteriorated, and the prices had diminished to a point where it would be a miracle if the food continued distinguished.

"Madame still conducts the restaurant?" I asked sharply.

I could now see that he was a Piedmontese of

the most evasive description. From rubbing his hands he had switched to twisting them.

"Not exactly," he said, "but we make the same cuisine."

I could not descry anything in the smudged ink but misspelled noodles and unorthographical *"escaloppinis"*; Italians writing French by ear produce a regression to an unknown ancestor of both languages.

"Try us," my man pleaded, and, like a fool, I did. I was hungry. Forty minutes later, I stamped out into the street as purple as an *aubergine* with rage. The minestrone had been cabbage scraps in greasy water. I had chosen *côtes d'agneau* as the safest item in the mediocre catalogue that the Prospéria's prospectus of bliss had turned into overnight. They had been cut from a tired Alpine billy goat and seared in machine oil, and the *haricots verts* with which they were served resembled decomposed whiskers from a theatrical-costume beard.

"The same cuisine?" I thundered as I flung my money on the falsified *addition* that I was too angry to verify. "You take me for a jackass!"

I am sure that as soon as I turned my back the scoundrel nodded. The restaurant has changed hands at least once since then.

In the morning, I telephoned Mirande. He confirmed the disaster. Mme. G., ill, had closed the restaurant. Worse, she had sold the lease and the good will, and had definitely retired.

"What is the matter with her?" I asked in a tone appropriate to fatal disease.

"I think it was trying to read Simone de Beauvoir," he said. "A syncope."

Mme. G. still lives, but Mirande is dead. When I met him in Paris the following November, his appearance gave no hint of decline. It was the season for his sable-lined overcoat *à l'impresario*, and a hat that was a furry cross between a porkpie and a homburg. Since the restaurant on the Rue Saint-Augustin no longer existed, I had invited him to lunch with me at a very small place called the Gratin Dauphinois, on the Rue Chabanais, directly across from the building that once housed the most celebrated sporting house in Paris. The Rue Chabanais is a short street that runs from the Square Louvois to the Rue des Petits Champs— perhaps a hundred yards—but before the reform wave stimulated by a Municipal Councilor named Marthe Richard at the end of the Second World War, the name Chabanais had a cachet all its own. Mme. Richard will go down in history as the Carry Nation of sex. Now the house is closed, and the premises are devoted to some low commercial purpose. The walls of the midget Gratin Dauphinois are hung with cartoons that have a nostalgic reference to the past glories of the street.

Mirande, when he arrived, crackled with jokes about the locale. He taunted me with being a criminal who haunts the scene of his misdeeds. The fare at the Gratin is robust, as it is in Dauphiné, but it did not daunt Mirande. The wine card, similarly, is limited to the strong, rough wines of Arbois and the like, with a couple of

Burgundies for clients who want to show off. There are no clarets; the proprietor hasn't heard of them. There are, of course, a few champagnes, for wedding parties or anniversaries, so Mirande, with Burgundies discounseled by his doctor, decided on champagne throughout the meal. This was a *drôle* combination with the mountain food, but I had forgotten about the lack of claret when I invited him.

We ordered a couple of dozen *escargots en pots de chambre* to begin with. These are snails baked and served, for the client's convenience, in individual earthenware crocks, instead of being forced back into shells. The snail, of course, has to be taken out of his shell to be prepared for cooking. The shell he is forced back into may not be his own. There is thus not even a sentimental justification for his reincarceration. The frankness of the service *en pot* does not improve the preparation of the snail, nor does it detract from it, but it does facilitate and accelerate his consumption. (The notion that the shell proves the snail's authenticity, like the head left on a woodcock, is invalid, as even a suburban housewife knows nowadays; you can buy a tin of snail shells in a supermarket and fill them with a mixture of nutted cream cheese and chopped olives.)

Mirande finished his dozen first, meticulously swabbing out the garlicky butter in each *pot* with a bit of bread that was fitted to the bore of the crock as precisely as a bullet to a rifle barrel. Tearing bread like that takes practice. We had emptied the first bottle of champagne when he placed his right hand delicately on the point of his waistcoat farthest removed from his spinal column.

"Liebling," he said, "I am not well."

It was like the moment when I first saw Joe Louis draped on the ropes. A great pity filled my heart. "*Maître*," I said, "I will take you home."

The dismayed *patronne* waved to her husband in the kitchen (he could see her through the opening he pushed the dishes through) to suspend the preparation of the *gendarme de Morteau*—the great smoked sausage in its tough skin—that we had proposed to follow the snails with. ("Short and broad in shape, it is made of pure pork and . . . is likely to be accompanied . . . by hot potato salad." —Root, page 217.) We had decided to substitute for the *pommes à l'huile* the *gratin dauphinois* itself. ("Thinly sliced potatoes are moistened with boiled milk and beaten egg, seasoned with salt, pepper, and nutmeg, and mixed with grated cheese, of the Gruyère type. The potatoes are then put into an earthenware dish which has been rubbed with garlic and then buttered, spotted with little dabs of butter, and sprinkled with more grated cheese. It is then cooked slowly in not too hot an oven." —Root, page 228.) After that, we were going to have a fowl in cream with *morilles*—wild black mushrooms of the mountains. We abandoned all.

I led Mirande into the street and hailed a taxi.

"I am not well, Liebling," he said. "I grow old."

He lived far from the restaurant, beyond the Place de l'Etoile, in the Paris of the successful.

From time to time on our way, he would say, "It is nothing. You must excuse me. I am not well."

The apartment house in which he and Mme. B. lived resembled one of the chic modern museums of the quarter, with entrance gained through a maze of garden patches sheathed in glass. Successive metal grilles swung open before us as I pushed buttons that Mirande indicated—in these modern palaces there are no visible flunkies—until we reached an elevator that smoothly shot us upward to his apartment, which was rather larger in area than the Square Louvois. The décor, with basalt columns and floors covered with the skin of jumbo Siberian tigers—a special strain force-fed to supply old-style movie stars—reminded me of the sets for *Belphégor,* a French serial of silent days that I enjoyed when I was a student at the Sorbonne in 1926. (It was, I think, about an ancient Egyptian high priest who came to life and set up bachelor quarters in Paris in the style of the Temple of Karnak.) Three or four maids rushed to relieve Mirande of his sable-lined coat, his hat, and his cane topped with the horn of an albino chamois. I helped him to a divan on which two Theda Baras could have defended their honor simultaneously against two villains of the silents without either couple's getting in the other's way. Most of the horizontal surfaces in the room were covered with sculpture and most of the vertical ones with large paintings. In pain though he was, Mirande called my attention to these works of art.

"All the sculptures are by Renoir," he said. "It

was his hobby. And all the paintings are by Maillol.
It was *his* hobby. If it were the other way around,
I would be one of the richest chaps in France.
Both men were my friends. But then, one doesn't
give one's friends one's bread and butter. And,
after all, it's less banal as it is."

After a minute, he asked me to help him to his
bedroom, which was in a wing of the apartment
all his own. When we got there, one of the maids
came in and took his shoes off.

"I am in good hands now, Liebling," he said.
"Farewell until next time. It is nothing."

I telephoned the next noon, and he said that his
doctor, who was a fool, insisted that he was ill.

Again I left Paris, and when I returned, late
the following January, I neglected Mirande. A
Father William is a comforting companion for
the middle-aged—he reminds you that the best is
yet to be and that there's a dance in the old dame
yet—but a sick old man is discouraging. My conscience stirred when I read in a gossip column in
France-Dimanche that Toto Mirande was con-
valescing nicely and was devouring caviar at a
great rate—with champagne, of course. (I had
never thought of Mirande as Toto, which is baby
slang for "little kid," but from then on I never
referred to him in any other way; I didn't want
anybody to think I wasn't in the know.) So the
next day I sent him a pound of fresh caviar from
Kaspia, in the Place de la Madeleine. It was the
kind of medication I approved of.

I received a note from Mirande by tube next
morning, reproaching me for spoiling him. He was

going better, he wrote, and would telephone in a day or two to make an appointment for a return bout. When he called, he said that the idiotic doctor would not yet permit him to go out to a restaurant, and he invited me, instead, to a family dinner at Mme. B.'s. "Only a few old friends, and not the cuisine I hope to give you at Maxim's next time," he said. "But one makes out."

On the appointed evening, I arrived early—or on time, which amounts to the same thing—*chez* Mme. B.; you take taxis when you can get them in Paris at the rush hours. The handsome quarter overlooking the Seine above the Trocadéro is so dull that when my taxi deposited me before my host's door, I had no inclination to stroll to kill time. It is like Park Avenue or the near North Side of Chicago. So I was the first or second guest to arrive, and Mme. B.'s fourteen-year-old daughter, by a past marriage, received me in the Belphégor room, apologizing because her mother was still with Toto—she called him that. She need not have told me, for at that moment I heard Madame, who is famous for her determined voice, storming at an unmistakable someone: "You go too far, Toto. It's disgusting. People all over Paris are kind enough to send you caviar, and because you call it monotonous, you throw it at the maid! If you think servants are easy to come by . . ."

When they entered the room a few minutes later, my old friend was all smiles. "How did you know I adore caviar to such a point?" he asked me. But I was worried because of what I had heard; the Mirande I remembered would never have been irritated by the obligation to eat a few extra kilos of fresh caviar. The little girl, who hoped I had not heard, embraced Toto. "Don't be angry with *Maman!*" she implored him.

My fellow guests included the youngish new wife of an old former Premier, who was unavoidably detained in Lille at a congress of the party he now headed; it mustered four deputies, of whom two formed a Left Wing and two a Right Wing. ("If they had elected a fifth at the last election, or if, by good luck, one had been defeated, they could afford the luxury of a Center," Mirande told me in identifying the lady. "*C'est malheureux,* a party without a Center. It limits the possibilities of maneuver.") There was also an amiable couple in their advanced sixties or beginning seventies, of whom the husband was the grand manitou of Veuve Clicquot champagne. Mirande introduced them by their right name, which I forget, and during the rest of the evening addressed them as M. and Mme. Clicquot. There was a forceful, black-haired man from the Midi, in the youth of middle age—square-shouldered, stocky, decisive, blatantly virile—who, I was told, managed Mme. B.'s vinicultural enterprises in Provence. There were two guests of less decided individuality, whom I barely remember, and filling out the party were the young girl—shy, carefully unsophisticated and unadorned—Mme. B., Mirande, and me. Mme. B. had a strong triangular face on a strong triangular base—a strong chin, high cheekbones, and a wide, strong jaw, but full of stormy good nature. She was a woman who, if she had been a man, would have wanted to be called Honest John. She had a high color and an iron handgrip, and repeatedly affirmed that there was no affectation about her, that she was *sans façon,* that she called her shots as she saw them. "I won't apologize," she said to me. "I know you're a great feeder, like Toto here, but I won't offer you the sort of menu he used to get in that restaurant you know of, where he ruined his plumbing. Oh, that woman! I used to be so jealous. I can offer only a simple home dinner." And she waved us toward a marble table about twenty-two feet long. Unfortunately for me, she meant it. The dinner began with a kidney-and-mushroom mince served in a giant popover—the kind of thing you might get at a literary hotel in New York. The inner side of the pastry had the feeling of a baby's palm, in the true tearoom tradition.

"It is savory but healthy," Madame said firmly, setting an example by taking a large second helping before starting the dish on its second round. Mirande regarded the untouched doughy fabric on his plate with diaphanously veiled horror, but he had an excuse in the state of his health. "It's still a little rich for me, darling," he murmured. The others, including me, delivered salvos of compliments. I do not squander my moral courage on minor crises. M. Clicquot said, "Impossible to obtain anything like this *chez* Lapérouse!" Mme. Clicquot said, "Not even at the Tour d'Argent!"

"And what do you think of my little wine?" Mme. B. asked M. Clicquot. "I'm so anxious for your professional opinion—as a rival producer, you know."

The wine was a thin *rosé* in an Art Nouveau bottle with a label that was a triumph of lithography; it had spires and monks and troubadours and blondes in wimples on it, and the name of the *cru* was spelled out in letters with Gothic curlicues and pennons. The name was something like Château Guillaume d'Aquitaine, *grand vin*.

"What a madly gay little wine, my dear!" M. Clicquot said, repressing, but not soon enough, a grimace of pain.

"One would say a Tavel of a good year," I cried, "if one were a complete bloody fool." I did not say the second clause aloud.

My old friend looked at me with new respect. He was discovering in me a capacity for hypocrisy that he had never credited me with before.

The main course was a shoulder of mutton with white beans—the poor relation of a gigot, and an excellent dish in its way, when not too dry. This was.

For the second wine, the man from the Midi proudly produced a red, in a bottle without a label, which he offered to M. Clicquot with the air of a tomcat bringing a field mouse to its master's feet. "Tell me what you think of this," he said as he filled the champagne man's glass.

M. Clicquot—a veteran of such challenges, I could well imagine—held the glass against the light, dramatically inhaled the bouquet, and then drank, after a slight stiffening of the features that indicated to me that he knew what he was in for. Having emptied half the glass, he deliberated.

"It has a lovely color," he said.

"But what is it? What is it?" the man from the Midi insisted.

"There are things about it that remind me of a Beaujolais," M. Clicquot said (he must have meant that it was wet), "but on the whole I should compare it to a Bordeaux" (without doubt unfavorably).

Mme. B.'s agent was beside himself with triumph. "Not one or the other!" he crowed. "It's from the *domaine*—the Château Guillaume d'- Aquitaine!"

The admirable M. Clicquot professed astonishment, and I, when I had emptied a glass, said that there would be a vast market for the wine in America if it could be properly presented. "Unfortunately," I said, "the cost of advertising . . ." and I rolled my eyes skyward.

"Ah, yes," Mme. B. cried sadly. "The cost of advertising!"

I caught Mirande looking at me again, and thought of the Pétrus and the Cheval Blanc of our last meal together *chez* Mme. G. He drank a glass of the red. After all, he wasn't going to die of thirst.

For dessert, we had a simple fruit tart with milk—just the thing for an invalid's stomach, although Mirande didn't eat it.

M. Clicquot retrieved the evening, oenologically, by producing two bottles of a wine "impossible to find in the cellars of any restaurant in France"— Veuve Clicquot '19. There is at present a great to-do among wine merchants in France and the United States about young wines, and an accompanying tendency to cry down the "legend" of the old. For that matter, hardware clerks, when you ask for a can opener with a wooden handle that is thick enough to give a grip and long enough for leverage, try to sell you complicated mechanical folderols. The motivation in both cases is the same—simple greed. To deal in wines of varied ages requires judgment, the sum of experience and flair. It involves the risk of money, because every lot of wine, like every human being, has a life span, and it is this that the good vintner must estimate. His object should be to sell his wine at its moment of maximum value—to the drinker as well as the merchant. The vintner who handles only young wines is like an insurance company that will write policies only on children; the unqualified dealer wants to risk nothing and at the same time to avoid tying up his money. The client misled by brochures warning him off clarets and champagnes that are over ten years old and assuring him that Beaujolais should be drunk green will miss the major pleasures of wine drinking. To deal wisely in wines and merely to sell them are things as different as being an expert in ancient coins and selling Indian-head pennies over a souvenir counter.

Despite these convictions of mine about wine, I should never have tried a thirty-seven-year-old champagne on the recommendation of a lesser authority than the blessed M. Clicquot. It is the oldest by far that I have ever drunk. (H. Warner

Allen, in *The Wines of France,* published circa 1924, which is my personal wine bible, says, "In the matter of age, champagne is a capricious wine. As a general rule, it has passed its best between fifteen and twenty, yet a bottle thirty years old may prove excellent, though all its fellows may be quite undrinkable." He cites Saintsbury's note that "a Perrier Jouet of 1857 was still majestical in 1884," adding, "And all wine-drinkers know of such amazing discoveries." Mr. Root, whose book is not a foolish panegyric of everything French, is hard on champagne, in my opinion. He falls into a critical error more common among writers less intelligent: he attacks it for not being something else. Because its excellences are not those of Burgundy or Bordeaux, he underrates the peculiar qualities it does not share with them, as one who would chide Dickens for not being Stendhal, or Marciano for not being Benny Leonard.)

The Veuve Clicquot '19 was tart without brashness—a refined but effective understatement of younger champagnes, which run too much to rhetoric, at best. Even so, the force was all there, to judge from the two glasses that were a shade more than my share. The wine still had a discreet *cordon*—the ring of bubbles that forms inside the glass—and it had developed the color known as "partridge eye." I have never seen a partridge's eye, because the bird, unlike woodcock, is served without the head, but the color the term indicates is that of serous blood or a maple leaf on the turn.

"How nice it was, life in 1919, eh, M. Clicquot?" Mirande said as he sipped his second glass.

After we had finished M. Clicquot's offering, we played a game called lying poker for table stakes, each player being allowed a capital of five hundred francs, not to be replenished under any circumstances. When Mme. B. had won everybody's five hundred francs, the party broke up. Mirande promised me that he would be up and about soon, and would show me how men reveled in the heroic days of *la belle époque*, but I had a feeling that the bell was cracked.

I left Paris and came back to it seven times during the next year, but never saw him. Once, being in his quarter in the company of a remarkably pretty woman, I called him up, simply because I knew he would like to look at her, but he was too tired. I forget when I last talked to him on the telephone. During the next winter, while I was away in Egypt or Jordan or someplace where French papers don't circulate, he died, and I did not learn of it until I returned to Europe.

When Mirande first faltered, in the Rue Chabanais, I had failed to correlate cause and effect. I had even felt a certain selfish alarm. If eating well was beginning to affect Mirande at eighty, I thought, I had better begin taking in sail. After all, I was only thirty years his junior. But after the dinner at Mme. B.'s, and in the light of subsequent reflection, I saw that what had undermined his constitution was Mme. G.'s defection from the restaurant business. For years, he had been able to escape Mme. B.'s solicitude for his health by lunching and dining in the restaurant of Mme. G., the sight of whom Mme. B. could not support. En-

tranced by Mme. G.'s magnificent food, he had
continued to live "like a cock in a pie"—eating as
well, and very nearly as much, as when he was
thirty. The organs of the interior—never very
intelligent, in spite of what the psychosomatic
quacks say—received each day the amount of
pleasure to which they were accustomed, and
never marked the passage of time; it was the indispensable roadwork of the prizefighter. When
Mme. G., good soul, retired, moderation began its
fatal inroads on his resistance. My old friend's
appetite, insufficiently stimulated, started to loaf
—the insidious result, no doubt, of the advice of
the doctor whose existence he had revealed to me
by that slip of the tongue about why he no longer
drank Burgundy. Mirande commenced, perhaps,
by omitting the fish course after the oysters, or the
oysters before the fish, then began neglecting his
cheeses and skipping the second bottle of wine on
odd Wednesdays. What he called his pipes (*"ma
tuyauterie"*), being insufficiently exercised, lost
their tone, like the leg muscles of a retired champion. When, in his kindly effort to please me, he
challenged the *escargots en pots de chambre,* he
was like an old fighter who tries a comeback without training for it. That, however, was only the
revelation of the rot that had already taken place.
What always happens happened. The damage was
done, but it could so easily have been averted had
he been warned against the fatal trap of absti-
nence.

II

Its Corollary

M. Mirande had
an equally rich life between meals. He had pleasure of women. Currently pleasure and women are
held matters incompatible, antithetical, and mu-
tually exclusive, like quinine water and Scotch.
Mirande also gave women pleasure; many women
had pleasure of him. This is no longer considered a
fair or honorable exchange. Women resent being
thought of as enjoyables; they consider such an
attitude an evidence of male chauvinism. They
want to be taken seriously, like fall-out.

The function of the sexes, if I read the authors
of the age aright, is mutual boredom.

It has become customary to write freely of the
sexual connection; but always with solemnity. One
may respectably write of his sexual initiation, provided it was a disaster. Holden Caulfield never got

to the post. Henry Miller may write about revelers self-woven into a human hooked rug, because his ecstasy is solemn. (Arriving in Paris at thirty-nine, he wrote about *la noce* like a child making a belated discovery of the banana split.) *Lady Chatterley's Lover* is acceptable because it is "a *serious* work of art." It is impossible, for the best of reasons, to prove it is a work of art, but it is easy to show that it is serious, the legalizing word. The jocund work of art is still beyond the pale. This is no damn joke.

The wretched how-to-do-it books about copulation are serious in intention, solemn in tone; the do-it-yourselfs will soon be with us.

The one thing about the glorious diversion that is no longer written, or if still written never published, is that it remains the most amusing as well as the most instructive of human activities, and one of the most nearly harmless. The same thing has happened in France, and it used to enrage Mirande.

"If I were a *tapette* writing plays about incest instead of simple fornication, I would have been a member of the Académie for the last twenty years," he once said to me.

The Académie has made posthumous amends by electing to membership Marcel Achard, Mirande's friend and disciple, who is a comic writer. M. Achard inherited M. Mirande's library, which will never be on exhibition at the Bibliothèque Nationale.

Nevertheless, Mirande was devout; he was as regular in attendance at mass Sunday morning as at the races in the afternoon. I imagine the Sieur de Brantôme was a good Catholic too.

There is in Mirande's *Souvenirs* a bewitching account of his visit to the leading lady of one of his great hits shortly before the First World War. He had a habit then of renting magnificent furnished flats and getting locked out of them. With three or four shows running on the Boulevards each season, he made a great deal of money, but it came in irregular spurts, and he had costly tastes and gambled high. He always left landlords to the last in paying up. He loathed them.

In this particular hour before the dawn, returning from Maxim's, he found that an especially spiteful landlord had chosen that night to invoke the law against him. Mirande was in evening clothes and had no place to take them off. From a telephone in an all-night bar he called the actress. Could he come up and sleep? Fortunately she was alone; she said she would be delighted. He stayed the heeltap of the night and half the next day with her. There was no spare room.

Early in the afternoon they were awakened by the actress' maid, who was in a state of extreme agitation. She excused herself for disturbing them but said there was a grave emergency: a man in the drawing room who said he would remove all the furniture if her mistress did not pay his bill, long overdue. She presented an official-looking *facture,* impressively decorated with legal stamps.

This was a piece of business the cast of two regularly acted out for rich admirers who stayed overnight for the first time. The actress' role called for her to burst into tears after receiving her cue, denounce herself as a silly, extravagant woman, and appeal to the admirer to save her from disgrace in the eyes of the quarter. (The scenario provided Mirande with an idea for a first act.)

This time, however, the actress turned on her maid with contempt.

"Imbecile!" she cried. "Can't you see that this is my *author*?"

The notion of getting money out of an author being obviously imbecilic, the maid had no riposte.

"And besides, that envelope is getting pretty gray. Provide yourself with some new stationery before the next time. And go!"

It was the kind of situation that Mirande loved. He especially loved the actress for keeping in form by acting even on days without a matinee.

He would not have understood the battle of the sexes. He saw life as their kindly collaboration. When Mirande was a boy of seventeen, fresh from Lannion, older women—demidowagers in their twenties—made love to him and taught him. When he was a ripe man he returned the favor by making love to the young.

Mirande boasted that he was good to the last. An expeditionary to Hollywood in his green youth, at sixty, he returned with a full *tableau de chasse*, and at eighty, just before the closure of the restaurant of Mme. G., he was meditating another invasion.

"We Frenchmen made love with our brains," he once said to me.

"We others utilize the traditional material," I said. It was the only time I ever had him.

After I published my first study of Mirande in *The New Yorker* I received an avalanche of letters —at least a dozen—from English-reading admirers of the great man, adding reminiscences that would have increased his stature if it were possible to do so.

"After all, he was the lover of the great star X," a woman wrote to me, "and that is nothing to sneeze at."

"I once asked him how X was to make love to," she continued, and he said, 'She is as randy as a pregnant cat.' "

Achard told me that Mirande, like many abnormally productive authors, was lazy. He would accumulate as many advances as possible before honoring any of his commitments and would then wait until the day before first rehearsal before beginning to write. He was confident, from experience, that an idea would occur to him when he needed it.

"Once he waited a day too long and appeared at rehearsal with a number of sheets of paper that he would allow nobody to read because he said they were so scribbled that only he could make them out. He made up the play as he went along, starting from the title, and it was a great success—*My Friend's Wife*. You can imagine the plot. He was a genius."

M. Achard, seeing that I thought that a bit strong, defined his terms.

"You know what is a genius?" he inquired. "Jacques Deval has said it: 'A genius is an author who writes not always flops.'

"Mirande once said to me that he did not enjoy love with society women," he said, reverting to another aspect of our old friend's genius. "He said they kissed as if they were sipping *crême de menthe* through a straw."

III

Paris the First

My personal Paris is like Byblos in Lebanon, a pile of cities stacked in order of seniority, the oldest at the bottom. Byblos has its culinary associations, too, because the low strata are peppered with large casseroles containing skeletons of a people who boiled their dead and folded them. I know, because I have been told, that I was in Paris in 1907, when I was three, at a hotel on Cours-la-Reine, but I remember nothing about that earliest visit. The first Paris I remember was a colonnaded city, like a stage set of a street with one side perpetually cool shade and the other bright, hot sun. In the middle of the street there was a cuirassier, the nearest thing to a knight in armor I had seen outside a picture book, immense in his plastron and boots. He sat a horse with two tails, one in the usual place and one hanging from

the back of the man's helmet. This was the Rue de
Rivoli in the dog days of 1911, when my family
paused there on the way home to New York from
a holiday in Europe proper, or *odiosa*, a place
where the inhabitants spoke German, as did my
oppressors, the Frauleins. Fraulein, to me, had the
strong specific meaning of nursegirl. It was to be
years before I realized that it could be applied to
an unmarried woman not in service. Many Frauleins *in* service must have been married, but I
never thought of one as *Frau*. Frauleins were my
immemorial enemies, interposed between my parents and me, like wicked bailiffs between kind
barons and their serfs. They were the bad door-
keepers of a benign sultan. Without their officious
intervention, I was sure, I could have been with my
parents twenty-four hours a day, and they would
have been charmed to have me. There were two
incidents of the 1907 trip that I did remember in
1911, and remember still, but they happened in
Germany.

In Wiesbaden in 1907 a Fraulein named Martha
had dragged me at unforgettable speed, my feet
touching the ground only occasionally, through
what I remembered as a mile of streets, to see a
tall man in a white uniform with a cape, sitting
in a white automobile on some hideous *Platz*, surrounded by a cheering crowd. He was, she told me
in hysteric shrieks, the Kaiser. Her tone would
have been appropriate to announce the Second
Coming. Martha ranked in the Frauleinian dynasty
like Caligula among Roman emperors. She was one
of the worst. In Nuremberg that same summer she

had packed me off to the torture tower in the old keep to see the Iron Maiden, a hinged hollow figure lined with spikes. The guide-lecturer said that prisoners were put inside and then squashed and blinded simultaneously. I understand now that the Maiden was a fake, but it was a *German* fake. Then they showed me the mouth of the well down which the torturers used to drop the broken bodies. The guide held a lighted candle and Martha held me in her arms and let me look down. Then he chucked a stone in and we waited an impressively long time before we heard it hit the water.

"It happens to naughty children, too," Martha said.

She bought me a miniature Iron Maiden as a souvenir.

My wars against the Frauleins left me with a blurred recollection of injustice and struggle, like the collective memory of the Irish, for whom I have an anomalous sympathy at their most difficult. We are like the children of long, hard deliveries, incredulous of our freedom even when we reach the clear. The Fraulein, I have thought often since, was a remarkably effective device for siphoning off from the parents the hostility that analysts assure us is the parents' due. Careful bootleggers in Harlem during Prohibition used to pass suspect alcohol through an old felt hat, on the theory that the poison would remain there. The Fraulein had the function of the felt hat. As full of the discharged hostility as the hat was of fusel oil, she shifted to another job when the child outgrew her. She left it as harmless to its parents as a baby rattlesnake milked of venom. To the child who began conscious life under the rule of a Fraulein, even the least bearable mother appeared an angel.

The device seems to me, looking back, more sensible than that of the kind nanny described in English novels. The nannies siphon off not the hostility, but the affection, leaving the protagonists incapable of liking anybody else for the rest of their lives. (Anticipating that these notes will be utilized at some future date by biographers, some analytically oriented, I shall make their path clearer by expositions like the above from time to time.)

It never occurred to me to wonder why my parents paid the Frauleins who deprived them of the pleasure of my constant company. I was sure the witches, like those in the fairy tales with which they tried to terrify me, had imposed themselves on the kind king and queen by some cunning swindle. We had a Fraulein with us even in Paris, although, to defend my pride, I insisted she was there only to take care of my sister, who was two and change. I was nearly seven. In fact, though, Fraulein had authority over me, too, especially in my parents' absences. I was only fourth in the chain of command, and my sister, the only member of the party I outranked, was too dumb to take orders from me.

France was better than Europe proper, because it was on the way home from it. The language sounded better, although I couldn't understand what people said in it. We lived at the Hotel

Regina, where the Place des Pyramides debouches into the Rue de Rivoli, and when we went out on foot we stayed under the colonnade because of the heat. We seldom got beyond the Place de la Concorde, because my sister, who in later years became as nimble as a roebuck, could not then walk worth a damn. For years afterward I thought of Paris as a city mostly roofed over, like a *souk*. I don't know why I think of the cuirassier as a permanent feature of the set. There may have been a fixed guard in front of one of the hotels because a visiting royal personage or head of state was in residence. But it is possible that I saw the soldier only once, and was so impressed that I never forgot him.

My parents abandoned the three of us often and went out into unroofed regions in a fiacre or a taxi. Hippomobile and automobile ages overlapped; it was no longer dashing to motor, nor yet quaint to prefer a carriage. My own prejudice in favor of horses was so strong that when I chanced to be with my parents they deferred to it.

All of us had stayed four weeks at Marienbad, a spa in Bohemia that is now known by some Slavic name, while Mother reduced her weight. Having reduced, she had an excuse to gather a wardrobe for her new figure before we went home. (She was sure to put the weight back on before the *Kaiserin Augusta Victoria* docked in Hoboken, nine days after leaving Cherbourg, but the dresses could always be let out.) Father had to accompany her to see how pretty she looked and to authorize expenditures that he would have rejected in horror if he had not been there to see her. He was not only proud of her looks—"A regular Lillian Russell," he would say—but sensitive to the good opinion of the mannequins and *vendeuses*. The sight of a pretty woman had an airborne chemical effect, like nerve gas. It relaxed the rubber band around his wallet. He was, moreover, helpless in Paris without Mother because he did not have French and thought she was fluent in it. It was an illusion she maintained as long as they traveled together.

"If you talk English to them they double the price," he used to say.

He did not suffer from this disadvantage in Europa Odiosa, since he spoke German, but it gave him little pleasure. What I principally remember him talking about in Marienbad was how a waiter captain had tried to swindle us by putting twenty-three rolls on our breakfast bill when we had taken only twenty-one. Mother, when on a diet, limited herself to three rolls.

Once that summer they took me, unforgettably, to Napoleon's tomb, where the gold light, the marble, and the massed battle flags made an image of Napoleonic glory that has always helped me understand the side of Stendhal that is least rational. If brief exposure to the glories of the Empire, a hundred years later, could so dazzle me, I find it easy to pardon the effect upon a lieutenant of dragoons eighteen years old, riding in the midst of the Sixth Light Dragoons, uniform bottle-green, red waistcoat, white breeches, helmet with crest, horsetail, and red cockade.

Napoleon's name and general repute were al-

ready known to me. He was a deity of the small
personal Olympus I was putting together for myself, like a collection of the pictures of baseball
players that then came in packages of cigarettes.
The captain of the team was George Washington,
and there were also Miss Russell (Aphrodite) and
Enrico Caruso (Pan). Washington was Zeus, or
boss god. His stern virtue—"I cannot tell a lie"—
put him above me and everybody else I knew, because we all lied frequently. His hatchet inspired
a terror I could not then explain to myself. I can
see now that his craggy *old* face under the white
hair—I had no notion then that he wore a pow-
dered wig—equated him with the Old Man of the
Tribe, or father-persona, vested with power symbolized by the ax. He looked mean enough to use it.
The cherry tree, of course, is a son-substitute—
Isaac is to Abraham as cherry tree to Washington
—and even the merest fool can see what the candied cherries are, symbolically speaking. (The
show windows of the Platt-Deutsch and Greek
confectionery stores in New York were full of
candied cherries, cardboard or chocolate hatchets,
and cardboard cherry trees, bearing edible cherries, for a week before Washington's birthday.
Here we have the personae and materia of a cult,
with a built-in miracle play.) I knew Miss Russell,
like Washington, only by hearsay. In my cos-
mogony she was already a figure of the past, associated with my prehistory and my parents' salad
days, because they talked about her that way. I was
astonished, on checking her dates when I wrote
this, to read that she retired from the stage only in

1912, at the age of fifty-one. In 1911, although no longer in perihelion, she was an undefeated champion still, about to retire into wealthy marriage with a Pittsburgh publisher. Miss Russell had been the reigning American Beauty, on and off stage, since about 1885. She was a butterscotch sundae of a woman, as beautiful as a tulip of beer with a high white collar. If a Western millionaire, one of the Hearst or Mackay kind, could have given an architect carte blanche to design him a woman, she would have looked like Lillian. She was San Simeon in corsets.

Mother, who was seventeen years younger, had bloomed in an age when all blond little girls with blue eyes wanted to grow up to be Lillian Russells. At puberty, if the girls were still pretty, their relatives began to compare them to their model.

Miss Russell embodied a style. Her hats were famously enormous and beplumed, even in an era of big, feathered hats. In photographs she seems to be wearing a forest of ostrich plumes above a mesa with an underbrush of satin bows. Her contours did not encourage fasting among her imitators. In building up to a similar opulence, I suppose, a younger woman developed eating habits that were hard to curb after she reached the target figure. That may have been Mother's difficulty.

A popular dessert named for the star, the Lillian Russell, was a half cantaloupe holding about a pint and three quarters of ice cream. If an actress had a dish named after her now, the recipe would be four phenobarbital tablets and a jigger of Metrecal. The consecrated silhouette was an hour-glass. Hence, I imagine, rose a dietary dilemma. A woman had to eat to stay plump above and below the pinch and slender in between.

Corsets afforded only partial and painful aid. I remember, as a small child, that in the bathing pavilion at Far Rockaway, the women, before going out on the beach, would summon the locker man, a leathery old drunk, to pull the strings of their corsets tight. In cinching them up, he would sometimes place his bare foot in the small of a whaleboned back. They tipped him for doing them this violence. People then were willing to go to more pains than now in order to look nice. The women were not alone in this. Marshal Mannerheim in his *Memoirs* recalls that officers of the Russian Imperial Guard used to put on their doeskin trousers, sit in a bath, and then let them dry tight to the skin.

Miss Russell and her imitators held their beautiful chins high, to arch the neck and prevent wrinkles. It was no time for an undecided profile. Throats, arms and backs counted more points than they do today because women wore low-necked gowns more often. People dressed for the dress circle in the Metropolitan Opera House then, for example, where now they wear street clothes in the boxes. Merely well-off couples, like my parents, with no social pretensions, often dressed just to go to friends' houses for dinner. I can remember Mother pausing in my bedroom to show herself off on some of these occasions in a white gown with gold sequins or a lilac with silver. I agreed with Father that she was a regular Lillian Russell.

Miss Russell, as reflected in my mother, furnished my basic pattern of feminine beauty. But the type already trembled on the brink of the archaic in 1911, like silent films the year before sound came in. Irene Castle lurked just around the corner of history, light of foot, long-legged and sparse, and by the early twenties, when I began to look purposefully at females, I would not find a Russellinear woman anywhere. (To this sharp bend in the river of womanly morphology I sometimes attribute my insatiable nostalgia for the past: I have a fixation on a form of animal life that no longer exists.)

Caruso, the fourth in my pantheon, was a Disembodied Voice, which is an essential feature of the history of any religion. His, with which I was familiar, came out of the horn, shaped like a morning-glory, of our Victrola. I could not understand what he said, which made it more awesome. Mostly, it seems to me now, he sang "E Lucevan le Stelle." I can identify it, at fifty years' distance, by the place where Cavaradossi sobs. Caruso sobbed louder than any other tenor, and when he did, my father always said, "That's art. You can tell a real artist by touches like that."

Tosca, Father used to say, was the touchstone for sopranos, too. "When she lays Scarpia out and puts the candles by the corpse, you can tell whether she can act," he would say. "She's just stabbed him, you know, and then she gets superstitious."

The only reason I would have liked to go to the Metropolitan in person was to see the stabbing; I wondered how they managed the blood. The music, I judged from the phonograph records, was something one could easily have too much of. The description "a regular Caruso" was as valid praise as "a regular Lillian Russell," but neither meant that the person so qualified was literally a deity—just that the amateur could sing well, or that the girl was a peach. There had been a third god on the same level, but his foot had slipped.

"A regular Jim Jeffries" no longer meant, in 1911, what it had before 1910, when that Caucasian Colossus had lost to Jack Johnson. You couldn't very well say that a white boy was a regular Jack Johnson.

Caruso was also a Pan-god, or satyr. Everybody knew that he had once followed a woman into the monkey house at the Central Park Zoo and pinched her in the rear. The woman had had him arrested. The incident had filled headlines; it had become legend. Thirty years later I was to learn that it was a press agent's trick, put up to attract attention to the tenor's appearance in a new role, Rodolfo in *La Bohème.* But then it was a myth that I accepted as fully as the story of George Washington and the cherry tree. Caruso, again like Miss Russell, was a deity often made manifest to my parents, more worthy than myself. Home from the Opera, they talked about his tonsils as if they were my Uncle Mike's.

In those days the people of New York saw its gods in the flesh, on the stage of the Met or the Colonial Theatre, or strutting in front of Kid Mc-Coy's saloon, according to the departments over which they presided. They were not a reconstituted mess of dots on a screen.

Culture impinged on daily life. My father, when shaving, sang the Toreador's air from *Carmen* every morning while stropping his razor. I associated this habit of his with the Caruso cult, too, but erroneously. Father, like Escamillo, was a baritone. There was only one word in his version of the song, and that deformed by a feminine ending that he dragged in for euphony:

"To-reea-Dora" . . .

He sang the rest of the music to a devocabularized lyric—"Ta, ra, ta, ra, *tah*."

He could shave with a straight blade on a transatlantic liner in a storm. The electric razor fosters no comparable talents.

I do not denigrate my pantheon of fifty years ago. An aesthetic taste founded on the gold light in the tomb and Lillian Russell's figure and Caruso singing Cavaradossi—and Sousa's Band and the Buffalo Bill show—is bound to be big and rich. It can be pruned down afterward.

In the Paris evenings, Father and Mother dined *en ville*, leaving the three of us to take supper in our room. Fraulein and I would share some uninspiring dish like cold cuts or an omelet, and my sister would have consommé and a soft-boiled egg, which made her unhappy. This particular Fraulein was rather nice, the only one I remember without distaste. I had, in any case, attained an age that forbade the worst personal indignities. (The most annoying was when they got the wash rag into your ear, meanwhile pulling the lobe with their other hand, but the most publicly humbling was when they spit on a handkerchief and wiped a smudge off your nose.) This Fraulein was Volks-Deutsch, from northern Hungary, and looked more Hungarian than German, with a good figure, ruddy complexion, and heavy black eyebrows. The room waiter was an Alsatian and won her confidence by speaking German. On the first night we were there, though, when he came back for the dishes after my sister and I were in our beds, he showed he was just like all the other Frenchmen, Fraulein told my mother the next day. He got fresh. Thereafter, she told him to leave the dishes for the maid to collect next morning, and she barricaded the door with chairs.

"But what could he do to you, Fraulein?" I asked her.

We nagged the poor girl so, during those hot days, that Mother advised her to take us to Rumpelmayer's *confiserie* under the colonnade, near the Hotel Continental, for what we had seen advertised on a window card as an American ice-cream soda. Fraulein could build a whole day of peace around the excursion, keeping us in line during the morning by threatening not to take us if we weren't good, then making us have a nap after lunch as preparation for the treat. Afterward we might, if she was lucky, be sick, and she could put us to bed again.

The day came, and we went. Fraulein and I had the sodas, but they were not, in my opinion, up to the standard of the West Side of New York. Trying, at this long distance in time, to appraise the trouble, I do not think Rumpelmeyer's had a genuine soda-fountain pump to gas them up with. I suspect that famous *salon de thé* of slopping a bottle of Perrier over a parfait. Boys liked their sodas very gassy then, with a sharp, metallic bite that reminded me of the smell of a bicycle-repair shop. My sister was allowed, I suppose, to have some of the ice cream out of my soda. Then the waitress brought the bill. Fraulein, who had expected they would cost ten cents, like the ones at home, did not have enough French money with her to pay it.

There was a conference, made more memorable because Fraulein spoke no French, and they trusted nobody who spoke German. The allegorical statue of Strasbourg among the cities of France in the Place de la Concorde was draped permanently in black; it was knee-high in funeral wreaths. We had once walked that far. *La revanche* was in the air, like humidity. Finally, Fraulein and the management reached a *Konkordat:* she was to go back to the hotel and change some Austrian *Kronen*— Rumpelmayer's wouldn't. She was to take Norma, who was already howling, with her. I was to be left as collateral.

She explained the deal to me before she left. I did not like it; I proposed we leave Norma. She said patiently that the reason Rumpelmayer's was releasing her even temporarily was to get Norma out of there. I demanded a supplement of pastry on the principle of extra danger pay, but Fraulein said that the management would advance no further credit.

So there I sat, for what seemed the second seven

years of my life, my apprehension steadily growing, while she walked the couple of hundred yards
back to the Regina and took Norma to the bathroom and came back. Before she made it I decided
a dozen times that she wouldn't. When at last she
reappeared, she asked me not to tell my parents
what had happened, and I blackmailed her out of
an éclair.

It was a prophetic trauma. I have spent a large
aggregate portion of my life since in situations that
repeated the quarter hour at Rumpelmayer's, waiting for a loan to bail me out. No matter how sure
I am that the money will arrive, I have the same
anxiety. My first stay in hock should have infected
me with a horror of Paris forever, but it didn't, although I did not know how deeply I was in love.
There would come a time when, if I had compared
my life to a cake, the sojourns in Paris would have
represented the chocolate filling. The intervening
layers were plain sponge. But my infatuations do
not begin at first taste. I nibble, reflect, come back
for more, and find myself forever addicted.

I remember, from that first Paris, the gold light
in the Tomb, the cuirassier, and the *vespasiennes*
where no Fraulein could pursue me. Finally, there
were two toys that I bore off with me to the Kaiserin Augusta Victoria. One was a chef *legumier*
who hacked away at a carrot with a big knife—
another version, had I but recognized it, of the
George Washington myth. The other was a scale
fire engine with hose no thicker than vermicelli
through which I could pump real water.

The chef symbolized in my unconscious Paris,

ville gastronomique, and the engine with its squirt
Paris, *ville d'art.* The graphic arts had their origin
in the free patterns made in the snow by Ice Age
man with warm water. This accounts for the fact
that there have been few good women painters.
Lot's wife, who looked behind her, may have been
a pioneer, but we had a head start of several mil-
lion years.

The years from 1911 to 1924 were plain sponge,
yet that dull stratum clinched my allegiance. Nine-
teen-fourteen was the year of transition to Francophile from mere Germanophobe. On August 1,
Fraulein Germania's armies crossed the frontier,
and the "Marseillaise" became my favorite tune.
I was by that time already a compulsive newspaper
reader instead of a tentative one, as I had been in
1911. I counted on Papa Joffre and the cuirassier
to avenge my early indignities. Joffre's face reminded me of Santa Claus, a pleasant association,
although I had long ceased to believe. (When I
saw Santa Clauses on street corners, I knew I
would soon get a lot of presents, and it set up a
pleasant mood. When I see them now, I know I
will have to give a lot, and I am filled with bile.)
All through August, though, the French retreated.
The Germans—I forget when they became Huns
—advanced toward Rumpelmayer's and the Hotel
Regina. It was a personal humiliation, because in
America I was surrounded by German rooters.

We were quartered at a hotel called Schaefer's
in Lake Hopatcong, a hot summer resort in New
Jersey. Schaefer's was a German-American kind
of place, as much roadhouse as hotel, built on the

side of a hill, with a dark, cool bar on the lowest
level. There was a fruit machine in this crypt, and
I would play it every day, until I had lost the last
nickel I could wheedle or extort from my mother.
Then I would drink sarsaparilla and eat Swiss
cheese sandwiches on rye while I read the Waverly
Novels. The sarsaparilla and sandwiches went on
the bill. The novels came from a mission-oak book-
case in the hall outside the dining room. When
Fraulein—the Paris one was still with us—would
drive me into the distasteful fresh air, I would
walk down to a pier, sit down again, and fish for
perch. I never caught one big enough to eat.

The bar, aromatic of stale beer, presented an
aspect of Teutonic culture I could appreciate, and
my antipathy might have shaded into indifference
if the war hadn't started. When it did, though,
Otto, the bartender, and Fred and Karl, the waiters, began to crow offensively about their national
superiority to everybody else. The French, they
said, bewrayed themselves from fear, and the English were fairies. As I was a great reader of G. A.
Henty, this involved me on a second front.

Victory followed victory, and as the help's chests
swelled, Fraulein's bosom heaved with them. She
was an Austro-Hungarian subject, and an ally.
Karl was cockeyed and he pinched lady guests'
bottoms when he thought he could get away with
it. He had long hinted he was a remittance man,
and he now professed to have been an officer on a
U-boat. Fraulein looked at him otherwise than she
had upon the Alsatian waiter in Paris. My attitude
toward her was now ambivalent, for I had begun

to take a sneaking interest in women and half regretted that I no longer shared a room with her and Norma; I would have welcomed the opportunities for observation. I therefore resented Fraulein Fasching's interest in Karl. Patriotism, I sensed, could be employed for ulterior purposes. I told her that if he was so brave he should go home and join the navy. She explained that since the cowardly English held the sea he couldn't— he was breaking his heart over it. But it was hardly worth regretting, because even if there were boats going, the Germans and Austrians would win the war before Karl could get there. He was having his *Schnecke* and eating it. I longed for Joffre to turn the tables, but he looked to be two out and ten runs behind in the last half of the ninth inning. The Marne determined my second nationality forever. I became a Frenchman at one remove.

By that time, I think, we were back in our house at Far Rockaway, a boundary province of Greater New York on Long Island. Like all frontier dwellers I was chauvinistic, and I thought of people who lived across the street in Nassau County as hicks. It was a tall, gaunt house, painted dark green and darkened by oaks that stood too close. (Thirty years later I saw it again and it had been divided into flats.) There Fraulein, reeling under the shock of Joffre's and my combined attack, received fresh support from Louis, our houseman, a Tyrolese from Meran. He had been working as a waiter in another summer hotel while we were away.

Louis was as Pan-German as Fraulein. He predicted that the Marne was only a temporary set-back. The French were merely a kind of Wops—I would see. He had his own kind of frontier chauvinism—anti-Italian. He had an impressive trick of jumping out of a third-floor window, grabbing a limb of an oak tree, and swinging his way down by changing handholds, like a pre-Weiss-muller Tarzan.

I was then in 5B. The war enlisted me and filled my proxy life for four years. When it ended I was a sophomore in high school. I grew up in it, transferring in fantasy from the cuirassiers, when I saw cavalry wouldn't do, to the heroic poilus, defenders of Verdun. I served a brief period as an officer of heroic Senegalese, and a short bit with the heroic Escadrille Lafayette. I also did a turn as liaison with our gallant allies, the heroic Brusiloff's heroic Cossacks. It is more vivid to me, even now, than the following World War; that is because I saw it through the eyes of correspondents who knew how to use their imaginations. Each fall, when the offensives that had begun so optimistically bogged down, I would say to Fraulein and Louis, like a Dodger fan, "Wait till next year." It was no longer fun for Fraulein—her brother was a surgeon with the Austrian army in Galicia, and after the sinking of the *Lusitania* it was clear which side was out of favor here.

Then in the Verdun spring—1916—while I walked along the parapet of my trench to show my fellows the Huns couldn't shoot, I began to feel queer and got sent home from school. Mother put me to bed, and it shortly transpired that I had typhoid fever. I had caught it by eating oysters from polluted waters—they had not been sold as such, of course—and I soon drifted into delirium, where I stayed for weeks of combat service on several fronts I had not yet visited. I had a particularly arduous indefinite period as a Serbian army horse, being ferried across a river as one in a bunch of bananas. On arriving at the other side of the river I was presented at a formal review of cuirassiers, where General Nivelle, the heroic commander of Verdun's heroic defenders, decorated me with the Médaille Militaire, which he attached to my right horse-ear by a safety pin. I put the medal under my pillow.

I had two trained nurses who lived in the house and worked around the clock—my parents didn't think well of the local hospital. As I achieved a patchy lucidity, I became aware of Miss Galt and Miss McCarthy as nurses in a military hospital. (I had stopped being a horse, but still had the medal, safe under the pillow.) They were kind, but I was peevish, and they sometimes said the conventional things.

Once, then, when the fever had departed and they thought I was quite all right in the head again, I gagged or whimpered at some measure of therapy, and Miss McCarthy said, "Don't be a crybaby."

It roused the *grand decoré*, in me, and I yelped, "Crybaby? How do you think I got that medal under my pillow?"

"Medal under what pillow?" she asked.

I lifted myself on an elbow and turned the pillow over, but my decoration wasn't there.

I was never so disappointed in my heroic life.*

* Thirty-six years later, in 1952, I got a French decoration for the most disappointing of reasons: being a writer— I sometimes take it surreptitiously from its case and stare at it, pretending that I won it by jumping a horse over the bayonets of a British square at Waterloo and, once in, decapitating a Colonel the Honorable Something-or-Other, a Tory back-bencher in the House of Commons.

IV

Just Enough Money

If, as I was saying before I digressed, the first requisite for writing well about food is a good appetite, the second is to put in your apprenticeship as a feeder when you have enough money to pay the check but not enough to produce indifference to the size of the total. (I also meant to say, previously, that Waverley Root has a good appetite, but I never got around to it.) The optimum financial position for a serious apprentice feeder is to have funds in hand for three more days, with a reasonable, but not certain, prospect of reinforcements thereafter. The student at the Sorbonne waiting for his remittance, the newspaperman waiting for his salary, the free-lance writer waiting for a check that he has cause to believe is in the mail—all are favorably situated to learn. (It goes without saying that it is essential to

be in France.) The man of appetite who will stint
himself when he can see three days ahead has no
vocation, and I dismiss from consideration, as
manic, the fellow who will spend the lot on one
great feast and then live on fried potatoes until his
next increment; Tuaregs eat that way, but only because they never know when they are going to
come by their next sheep. The clear-headed vora-
cious man learns because he tries to compose his
meals to obtain an appreciable quantity of pleasure from each. It is from this weighing of delights
against their cost that the student eater (particularly if he is a student at the University of Paris)
erects the scale of values that will serve him until
he dies or has to reside in the Middle West for a
long period. The scale is different for each eater,
as it is for each writer.

Eating is highly subjective, and the man who
accepts say-so in youth will wind up in bad and
overtouted restaurants in middle age, ordering
what the maître d'hôtel suggests. He will have
been guided to them by food-snob publications,
and he will fall into the habit of drinking too much
before dinner to kill the taste of what he has been
told he should like but doesn't. An illustration: For
about six years, I kept hearing of a restaurant in
the richest shire of Connecticut whose proprietor,
a Frenchman, had been an assistant of a disciple
of the great Escoffier. Report had it that in these
wilds—inhabited only by executives of the highest
grade, walking the woods like the King of Nemi
until somebody came on from Winnetka to cut
their throats—the restaurateur gave full vent to

57

the creative flame. His clients took what he chose
to give them. It they declined, they had to go down
the pike to some joint where a steak cost only
twelve dollars, and word would get around that
they felt their crowns in danger—they had been
detected economizing. I finally arranged to be
smuggled out to the place disguised as a *Time-Life*
Executive Vice-Publisher in Charge of Hosannas
with the mission of entertaining the advertising
manager of the Hebrew National Delicatessen
Corporation. When we arrived, we found the Yale-
blue vicuña rope up and the bar full of couples in
the hundred-thousand-dollar bracket, dead drunk
as they waited for tables; knowing that this would
be no back-yard cookout, they had taken prophy-
lactic anesthesia. But when I tasted the food, I
perceived that they had been needlessly alarmed.
The Frenchman, discouraged because for four
years no customers had tasted what they were
eating, had taken to bourbon-on-the-rocks. In a
morose way, he had resigned himself to becoming
dishonestly rich. The food was no better than
Howard Johnson's, and the customers, had they
not been paralyzed by the time they got to it, would
have liked it as well. The *spécialité de la maison*,
the unhappy *patron* said when I interrogated him,
was jellied oysters dyed red, white, and blue. "At
least they are aware of that," he said. "The colors
attract their attention." There was an on-the-hour
service of Brink's armored cars between his door
and the night-deposit vault of a bank in New York,
conveying the money that rolled into the *caisse*.
The wheels, like a juggernaut's, rolled over his

secret heart. His intention in the beginning had been noble, but he was a victim of the system.

The reference room where I pursued my own first earnest researches as a feeder without the crippling handicap of affluence was the Restaurant des Beaux-Arts, on the Rue Bonaparte, in 1926-27. I was a student, in a highly generalized way, at the Sorbonne, taking targets of opportunity for study. Eating soon developed into one of my major subjects. The franc was at twenty-six to the dollar, and the researcher, if he had only a certain sum—say, six francs—to spend, soon established for himself whether, for example, a half bottle of Tavel *supérieur*, at three and a half francs, and braised beef heart and yellow turnips, at two and a half, gave him more or less pleasure than a *contre-filet* of beef, at five francs, and a half bottle of *ordinaire*, at one franc. He might find that he liked the heart, with its strong, rich flavor and odd texture, nearly as well as the beef, and that since the Tavel was overwhelmingly better than the cheap wine, he had done well to order the first pair. Or he might find that he so much preferred the generous, sanguine *contre-filet* that he could accept the undistinguished *picrate* instead of the Tavel. As in a bridge tournament, the learner played duplicate hands, making the opposite choice of fare the next time the problem presented itself. (It was seldom as simple as my example, of course, because a meal usually included at least an hors d'oeuvre and a cheese, and there was a complexity of each to choose from. The arrival, in season, of fresh asparagus or venison further complicated matters. In the first case, the investigator had to decide what course to omit in order to fit the asparagus in, and, in the second, whether to forgo all else in order to afford venison.)

A rich man, faced with this simple sumptuary dilemma, would have ordered both the Tavel *and* the *contre-filet*. He would then never know whether he liked beef heart, or whether an *ordinaire* wouldn't do him as well as something better. (There are people to whom wine is merely an alcoholized sauce, although they may have sensitive palates for meat or pastries.) When one considers the millions of permutations of foods and wines to test, it is easy to see that life is too short for the formulation of dogma. Each eater can but establish a few general principles that are true only for him. Our hypothetical rich *client* might even have ordered a Pommard, because it was listed at a higher price than the Tavel, and because he was more likely to be acquainted with it. He would then never have learned that a good Tavel is better than a fair-to-middling Pommard—better than a fair-to-middling almost anything, in my opinion. In student restaurants, renowned wines like Pommard were apt to be mediocre specimens of their kind, since the customers could never have afforded the going prices of the best growths and years. A man who is rich in his adolescence is almost doomed to be a dilettante at table. This is not because all millionaires are stupid but because they are not impelled to experiment. In learning to eat, as in psychoanalysis, the customer, in order to profit, must be sensible of the cost.

There is small likelihood that a rich man will frequent modest restaurants even at the beginning of his gustatory career; he will patronize restaurants, sometimes good, where the prices are high and the repertory is limited to dishes for which it is conventionally permissible to charge high prices. From this list, he will order the dishes that in his limited experience he has already found agreeable. Later, when his habits are formed, he will distrust the originality that he has never been constrained to develop. A diet based chiefly on game birds and oysters becomes a habit as easily as a diet of jelly doughnuts and hamburgers. It is a better habit, of course, but restrictive just the same. Even in Paris, one can dine in the costly restaurants for years without learning that there are fish other than sole, turbot, salmon (in season), trout, and the Mediterranean *rouget* and *loup de mer*. The fresh herring or sardine *sauce moutarde;* the *colin froid mayonnaise;* the conger eel *en matelote;* the small fresh-water fish of the Seine and the Marne, fried crisp and served *en buisson;* the whiting *en colère* (his tail in his mouth, as if contorted with anger); and even the skate and the *dorade*—all these, except by special and infrequent invitation, are out of the swim. (It is a standing tourist joke to say that the fishermen on the quays of the Seine never catch anything, but in fact they often take home the makings of a nice fish fry, especially in winter. In my hotel on the Square Louvois, I had a room waiter—a Czech naturalized in France—who used to catch hundreds of *goujons* and *ablettes* on his days off. He once brought a shoe box of them to my room to prove that Seine fishing was not pure whimsey.) All the fish I have mentioned have their habitats in humbler restaurants, the only places where the aspirant eater can become familiar with their honest fishy tastes and the decisive modes of accommodation that suit them. Personally, I like tastes that know their own minds. The reason that people who detest fish often tolerate sole is that sole doesn't taste very much like fish, and even this degree of resemblance disappears when it is submerged in the kind of sauce that patrons of Piedmontese restaurants in London and New York think characteristically French. People with the same apathy toward decided flavor relish "South African lobster" tails—frozen as long as the Siberian mammoth—because they don't taste lobstery. ("South African lobsters" are a kind of sea crayfish, or *langouste*, but that would be nothing against them if they were fresh.) They prefer processed cheese because it isn't cheesy, and synthetic vanilla extract because it isn't vanillary. They have made a triumph of the Delicious apple because it doesn't taste like an apple, and of the Golden Delicious because it doesn't taste like anything. In a related field, "dry" (non-beery) beer and "light" (non-Scotchlike) Scotch are more of the same. The standard of perfection for vodka (no color, no taste, no smell) was expounded to me long ago by the then Estonian consul-general in New York, and it ac-

counts perfectly for the drink's rising popularity
with those who like their alcohol in conjunction
with the reassuring tastes of infancy—tomato
juice, orange juice, chicken broth. It is the ideal
intoxicant for the drinker who wants no reminder
of how hurt Mother would be if she knew what he
was doing.

The consistently rich man is also unlikely to
make the acquaintance of meat dishes of robust
taste—the hot *andouille* and *andouillette*, which
are close-packed sausages of smoked tripe, and the
boudin, or blood pudding, and all its relatives that
figure in the pages of Rabelais and on the menus
of the market restaurants. He will not meet the
civets, or dark, winy stews of domestic rabbit and
old turkey. A tough old turkey with plenty of
character makes the best *civet,* and only in a *civet*
is turkey good to eat. Young turkey, like young
sheep, calf, spring chicken, and baby lobster, is a
pale preliminary phase of its species. The pig, the
pigeon, and the goat—as suckling, squab, and kid
—are the only animals that are at their best to
eat when immature. The first in later life becomes gross through indolence; the second and
third grow muscular through overactivity. And the
world of tripery is barred to the well-heeled, except
for occasional exposure to an expurgated version
of *tripes à la mode de Caen.* They have never seen
gras-double (tripe cooked with vegetables, principally onions) or *pieds et paquets* (sheep's tripe
and calves' feet with salt pork). In his book, Waverley Root dismisses tripe, but he is no plutocrat;
his rejection is deliberate, after fair trial. Still, his

insensibility to its charms seems to me odd in a
New Englander, as he is by origin. Fried pickled
honeycomb tripe used to be the most agreeable
feature of a winter breakfast in New Hampshire,
and Fall River, Root's home town, is in the same
cultural circumscription.

Finally, to have done with our rich man, seldom
does he see even the simple, well-pounded *bifteck*
or the *pot-au-feu* itself—the foundation glory of
French cooking. Alexandre Dumas the elder wrote
in his *Dictionary Cuisine:* "French cooking, the
first of all cuisines, owes its superiority to the excellence of French bouillon. This excellence de-
rives from a sort of intuition with which I shall not
say our cooks but our women of the people are
endowed." This bouillon is one of the two end prod-
ucts of the *pot.* The other is the material that has
produced it—beef, carrots, parsnips, white turnips,
leeks, celery, onions, cloves, garlic, and cracked
marrowbones, and, for the dress version, fowl.
Served *in* some of the bouillon, this constitutes the
dish known as *pot-au-feu.* Dumas is against poultry "unless it is old," but advises that "an old
pigeon, a partridge, or a rabbit roasted in advance,
a crow in November or December" works wonders.
He postulates "seven hours of sustained simmering," with constant attention to the "scum" that
forms on the surface and to the water level.
("Think twice before adding water, though if your
meat actually rises above the level of the bouillon
it is necessary to add boiling water to cover it.")
This supervision demands the full-time presence
of the cook in the kitchen throughout the day, and

the maintenance of the temperature calls for a considerable outlay in fuel. It is one reason that the *pot-au-feu* has declined as a chief element of the working-class diet in France. Women go out to work, and gas costs too much. For a genuinely good *pot-au-feu,* Dumas says, one should take a fresh piece of beef—"a twelve-to-fifteen-pound rump"—and simmer it seven hours in the bouillon of the beef that you simmered seven hours the day before. He does not say what good housekeepers did with the first piece of beef—perhaps cut it into sandwiches for the children's lunch. He regrets that even when he wrote, in 1869, excessive haste was beginning to mar cookery; the demanding ritual of the *pot* itself had been abandoned. This was "a receptacle that never left the fire, day or night," Dumas writes. "A chicken was put into it as a chicken was withdrawn, a piece of beef as a piece was taken out, and a glass of water whenever a cup of broth was removed. Every kind of meat that cooked in this bouillon gained, rather than lost, in flavor." *Pot-au-feu* is so hard to find in chic restaurants nowadays that every Saturday evening there is a mass pilgrimage from the fashionable quarters to Chez Benoit, near the Châtelet—a small but not cheap restaurant that serves it once a week. I have never found a crow in Benoit's *pot,* but all the rest is good.

A drastically poor man, naturally, has even less chance than a drastically rich one to educate himself gastronomically. For him eating becomes merely a matter of subsistence; he can exercise no choice. The chief attraction of the cheapest student restaurants in my time was advertised on their largest placards: *"Pain à Discrétion"* ("All the Bread You Want"). They did not graduate discriminating eaters. During that invaluable year, I met a keen observer who gave me a tip: "If you run across a restaurant where you often see priests eating with priests, or sporting girls with sporting girls, you may be confident that it is good. Those are two classes of people who like to eat well and get their money's worth. If you see a priest eating with a layman, though, don't be too sure about the money's worth. The fellow *en civil* may be a rich parishioner, and the good Father won't worry about the price. And if the girl is with a man, you can't count on anything. It may be her kept man, in which case she won't care what she spends on him, or the man who is keeping her, in which case she won't care what he spends on her."

Failing the sure indications cited above, a good augury is the presence of French newspapermen.

The Restaurant des Beaux-Arts, where I did my early research, was across the street from the Ecole des Beaux-Arts, and not, in fact, precisely in my quarter, which was that of the university proper, a good half mile away, on the other side of the Boulevard Saint-Germain. It was a half mile that made as much difference as the border between France and Switzerland. The language was the same, but not the inhabitants. Along the Rue Bonaparte there were antiquarians, and in the streets leading off it there were practitioners of the ancillary arts—picture framers and bookbinders. The bookshops of the Rue Bonaparte, of which there were many, dealt in fine editions and rare books, instead of the used textbooks and works of erudition that predominated around the university. The students of the Beaux-Arts were only a small element of the population of the neighborhood, and they were a different breed from the students of the Boulevard Saint-Michel and its tributaries, such as the Rue de l'Ecole de Médecine, where I lived. They were older and seemingly in easier circumstances. I suspected them of commercial art and of helping Italians to forge antiques. Because there was more money about, and because the quarter had a larger proportion of adult, experienced eaters, it was better territory for restaurants than the immediate neighborhood of the Sorbonne. I had matriculated at the Faculté des Lettres and at the Ecole des Chartes, which forms medievalists, but since I had ceased attending classes after the first two weeks, I had no need to stick close to home. One of the chief joys of that academic year was that it was one long cut without fear of retribution.

I chanced upon the Restaurant des Beaux-Arts while strolling one noon and tried it because it looked neither chic nor sordid, and the prices on the menu were about right for me: *pâté maison,* 75 centimes; sardines, 1 franc; artichoke, 1.25; and so on. A legend over the door referred to the proprietor as a M. Teyssedre, but the heading of the bill of fare called him Balazuc. Which name represented a former proprietor and which the current one I never learned. I had a distaste for asking direct questions, a practice I considered ill-bred. This had handicapped me during my brief career as a reporter in Providence, Rhode Island, but not as much as you might think. Direct questions tighten a man up, and even if he answers, he will not tell you anything you have not asked him. What you want is to get him to tell you his story. After he has, you can ask clarifying questions, such as "How did you come to have the ax in your hand?" I had interrupted this journalistic grind after one year, at the suggestion of my father, a wise man. "You used to talk about wanting to go to Europe for a year of study," he said to me one spring day in 1926, when I was home in New York for a weekend. "You are getting so interested in what you are doing that if you don't go now you never will. You might even get married."

I sensed my father's generous intention, and, fearing that he might change his mind, I told him that I didn't feel I should go, since I was indeed thinking of getting married. "The girl is ten years older than I am," I said, "and Mother might think she is kind of fast, because she is being kept by a cotton broker from Memphis, Tennessee, who only comes North once in a while. But you are a man of the world, and you understand that a woman can't always help herself. Basically . . ." Within the week, I had a letter of credit on the Irving Trust for two thousand dollars, and a reservation on the old *Caronia* for late in the summer, when the off-season rates would be in effect. It was characteristic of my father that even while doing a remarkably generous thing he did not want to waste the difference between a full-season and an off-season passage on a one-class boat. (He never called a liner anything but a boat, and I always found it hard to do otherwise myself, until I stopped trying. "Boat" is an expression of affection, not disrespect; it is like calling a woman a girl. What may be ships in proportion to Oxford, where the dictionary is written, are boats in proportion to New York, where they nuzzle up to the bank to feed, like the waterfowl in Central Park.)

While I continued to work on the Providence paper until the rates changed, Father, with my mother and sister, embarked for Europe on a Holland-American boat—full-season rate and first class—so that my sister might take advantage of her summer holiday from school. I was to join them for a few days at the end of the summer, after which they would return to the United States and I would apply myself to my studies. Fortunately, I discovered that the titulary of a letter of credit can draw on it at the issuing bank as easily as abroad. By the time I sailed, I was eight hundred dollars into the letter, and after a week in Paris at a hotel off the Champs-Elysées I found, without astonishment, that I had spent more than half of the paternal fellowship that was intended to last me all year. The academic year would not begin until November, and I realized that I would be lucky to have anything at all by then. At this juncture, the cotton broker's girl came to my rescue in a vision, as an angel came to Constantine's. I telegraphed to my parents, who were at Lake Como, that I was on my way to join them. From my attitude when I got there—reserved, dignified, preoccupied—my father sensed that I was in trouble. The morning after my arrival, I proposed that we take a walk, just the two of us, by the lake. Soon we felt thirst, and we entered the trellised arbor of a hotel more modest than ours and ordered a bottle of rustic wine that recalled the stuff that Big Tony, my barber in Providence, used to manufacture in his yard on Federal Hill. Warmed by this homelike glow, I told my father that I had dilapidated his generous gift; I had dissipated in riotous living seventy-two per cent of the good man's unsolicited benefaction. Now there was only one honorable thing for me to do—go back to work, get married, and settle down. "She is so noble that she wouldn't tell me," I said, "but I'm afraid I left her in the lurch."

"God damn it," he said, "I knew I should never have given you that money in one piece. But I want you to continue your education. How much will you need every month?"

"Two hundred," I said, moderately. Later, I wished I had asked for fifty more; he might have gone for it. "You stay in Paris," he said—he knew I had chosen the Sorbonne—"and I'll have the Irving send you two hundred dollars every month. No more lump sums. When a young man gets tangled up with that kind of women, they can ruin his whole life."

That was how I came to be living in Paris that academic year in a financial situation that facilitated my researches. Looking back, I am sure my father knew that I wanted to stay on, and that there was no girl to worry about. But he also understood that I couldn't simply beg; for pride's sake, I had to offer a fake *quid pro quo* and pretend to myself that he believed me. He had a very good idea of the value of leisure, not having had any until it was too late to become accustomed to it, and a very good idea of the pleasure afforded by knowledge that has no commercial use, having never had time to acquire more than a few odd bits. His parents had brought him to America when he was eight years old; he went to work at ten, opened his own firm at twenty-one, started being rich at thirty, and died broke at sixty-five— a perfect Horatio Alger story, except that Alger never followed his heroes through. At the moment, though, he had the money, and he knew the best things it would buy.

The great day of each month, then, was the one when my draft arrived at the main office of the Crédit Lyonnais—the Irving's correspondent bank —on the Boulevard des Italiens. It was never even approximately certain what day the draft would get there; there was no air mail, and I could not be sure what ship it was on. The Crédit, on receiving the draft, would notify me, again by ordinary mail, and that would use up another day. After the second of the month, I would begin to be haunted by the notion that the funds might have arrived and that I could save a day by walking over and inquiring. Consequently, I walked a good many times across the river and the city from the Rue de l'Ecole de Médecine to the Boulevard des Italiens, via the Rue Bonaparte, where I would lunch at the Maison Teyssedre or Balazuc. There were long vertical black enamel plaques on either side of the restaurant door, bearing, in gold letters, such information as "Room for Parties," "Telephone," "Snails," "Specialty of Broils," and, most notably, "Renowned Cellar, Great Specialty of Wines of the Rhone." The Great Specialty dated back to the regime of a proprietor anteceding M. Teyssedre-Balazuc. This prehistoric *patron*, undoubtedly an immigrant from Languedoc or Provence, had set up a bridgehead in Paris for the wines of his region of origin.

The wines of the Rhone each have a decided individuality, viable even when taken in conjunction with *brandade de morue*—a delightful purée of salt codfish, olive oil, and crushed garlic— which is their compatriot. *Brandade*, according to Root, is "definitely not the sort of dish that is likely to be served at the Tour d'Argent." "Subtlety," that hackneyed wine word, is a cliché seldom employed in writing about Rhone wines; their appeal is totally unambiguous. The Maison Teyssedre-Balazuc had the whole gamut, beginning with a rough, faintly sour Côtes du Rhône—which means, I suppose, anything grown along that river as it runs its three-hundred-and-eighty-mile course through France. It continued with a Tavel and then a Tavel *supérieur*. The proprietor got his wines in barrel and bottled them in the Renowned Cellar; the plain Tavel came to the table in a bottle with a blue wax seal over the cork, the *supérieur* in a bottle with a purple seal. It cost two cents more a pint. I do not pretend to remember every price on the card of the Restaurant des Beaux-Arts, but one figure has remained graven in my heart like "Constantinople" in the dying Czar's. A half bottle of Tavel *supérieur* was 3.50; I can still see the figure when I close my eyes, written in purple ink on the cheap, grayish paper of the *carte*. This is a mnemonic testimonial to how good the wine was, and to how many times I struggled with my profligate tendencies at that particular point in the menu, arguing that the unqualified Tavel, which was very good, was quite good enough; two cents a day multiplied by thirty, I frequently told myself, mounted up to fifteen francs a month. I don't think I ever won the argument; my spendthrift palate carried the day. Tavel has a rose-cerise *robe*, like a number of well-known racing silks, but its taste is not thin or acidulous, as that of most of its mimics is. The taste is warm but dry, like an enthusiasm held under restraint, and there is a tantalizing suspicion of bitterness when the wine hits the top of the palate. With the second glass, the enthusiasm gains; with the third, it is overpowering. The effect is generous and calorific, stimulative of cerebration and the social instincts. "An apparently light but treacherous *rosé*," Root calls it, with a nuance of resentment that hints at some old misadventure.

Tavel is from a place of that name in Languedoc, just west of the Rhone. In 1926, there were in all France only two well-known wines that were neither red nor white. One was Tavel, and the other Arbois, from the Jura—and Arbois is not a rose-colored but an "onion-peel" wine, with russet and purple glints. In the late thirties, the *rosés* began to proliferate in wine regions where they had never been known before, as growers discovered how marketable they were, and to this day they continue to pop up like measles on the wine map. Most often *rosés* are made from red wine grapes, but the process is abbreviated by removing the liquid prematurely from contact with the grape skins. This saves time and trouble. The product is a semi-aborted red wine. Any normally white wine can be converted into a *rosé* simply by adding a dosage of red wine* or cochineal.

In 1926 and 1927, for example, I never heard of Anjou *rosé* wine, although I read wine cards every day and spent a week of purposeful drinking in Angers, a glorious white-wine city. Alsace is another famous white-wine country that now lends its name to countless cases of a pinkish cross between No-Cal and vinegar; if, in 1926, I had crossed the sacred threshold of Valentin Sorg's restaurant in Strasbourg and asked the sommelier for a *rosé d'Alsace*, he would have, quite properly, kicked me into Germany. The list is endless now; flipping the coated-paper pages of any dealer's brochure, you see *rosés* from Bordeaux, Burgundy, all the South of France, California, Chile, Algeria, and heaven knows where else. Pink champagne, colored by the same procedure, has existed for a century and was invented for the African and Anglo-Saxon trade. The "discovery" of the demand for pink wine approxi-

* "Some [peasants] will give you a quick recipe for *rosé* which shall not pollute these pages."—The late Morton Shand's classic, *A Book of French Wines*, Jonathan Cape, Ltd., London, 1960 edition.

mately coincided with the repeal of prohibition in the United States. (The American housewife is susceptible to eye and color appeal.) In England, too, in the same period, a new class of wine buyer was rising with the social revolution. Pink worked its miracle there, and also in France itself, where many families previously limited to the cheapest kind of bulk wine were beginning to graduate to "nice things."

Logically, there is no reason any good white- or red-wine region should not produce equally good *rosé*, but in practice the proprietors of the good vineyards have no cause to change the nature of their wines; they can sell every drop they make. It is impossible to imagine a proprietor at Montrachet, or Chablis, or Pouilly, for example, tinting his wine to make a Bourgogne *rosé*. It is almost as hard to imagine it of a producer of first-rate Alsatian or Angevin wines. The wines converted to *rosé* in the great-wine provinces are therefore, I suspect, the worst ones—a suspicion confirmed by almost every experience I have had of them. As for the *rosés* from the cheap-wine provinces they are as bad as their coarse progenitors, but are presented in fancy bottles of untraditional form— a trick learned from the perfume industry. The bottles are generally decorated with art labels in the style of Robida's illustrations for Rabelais, and the wines are peddled at a price out of all proportion to their inconsiderable merits. There is also behind their gruesome spread the push of a report, put out by some French adman, that while white wine is to be served only with certain aliments, and red wine only with certain others, *rosé* "goes with everything," and so can be served without embarrassment by the inexperienced hostess. The truth is, of course, that if a wine isn't good it doesn't "go" with anything, and if it is it can go in any company.* Tavel though, is the good, the old, and, as far as I am concerned, still the only worthy *rosé*.†

At the Restaurant des Beaux-Arts, the Tavel *supérieur* was as high on the list as I would let my eyes ascend until I felt that the new money was on its way. When I had my first supersensory intimation of its approach, I began to think of the prizes higher on the card—Côte Rôtie, Châteauneuf-du-Pape, and white as well as red Hermitage, which cost from three to five francs more, by the half bottle, than my customary Purple Seal. Racing men like to say that a great horse usually has a great name—impressive and euphonious—and these three wines bear similar cachets. The Pope's

---

* Mr. Frank Schoonmaker, a writer on wine and a dealer in it who has done much to diffuse *rosé* in this country, wrote to me after the first appearance of this statement that I "surely wouldn't want to serve a good claret with sardine or a Montrachet with roast beef." To this I must answer that I wouldn't serve a Montrachet or any other good wine of *any* color with sardines, since they would make it taste like more sardines. Beer might be a better idea, or in its default, *rosé*, and I offer, without charge, the advertising slogan "*Rosé,* the perfect companion for fish oil."

† The eminent Shand, in 1960 (*A Book of French Wines*), wrote with more authority but no less bitterness of the Pink Plague: "Odd little *rosés* were belatedly exhumed from a more than provincial obscurity to set before clamorous foreign holiday parties; or if none such had ever existed steps were speedily taken to produce a native *rosé*."

new castle and the Hermitage evoke medieval pomp and piety, but the name Côte Rôtie—the hillside roasted in the sun—is the friendliest of the three, as is the wine, which has a cleaner taste than Châteauneuf and a warmer one than Hermitage. Châteauneuf often seems to be a wine that there is too much of to be true, and it varies damnably in all respects save alcoholic content, which is high. Red Hermitage is certainly distinguished; as its boosters like to say, of all Rhone wines it most resembles a great Burgundy, but perhaps for that reason it was hardest for a young man to understand. It was least like a *vin du Rhône.* As for the scarce white Hermitage, of which I haven't encountered a bottle in many years, it left a glorious but vague memory. Côte Rôtie was my darling. Drinking it, I fancied I could see that literally roasting but miraculously green hillside, popping with goodness, like the skin of a roasting duck, while little wine-colored devils chased little nymphs along its simmering rivulets of wine. (Thirty years later, I had a prolonged return match with Côte Rôtie, when I discovered it on the wine card of Prunier's, in London. I approached it with foreboding, as you return to a favorite author whom you haven't read for a long time, hoping that he will be as good as you remember. But I need have had no fear. Like Dickens, Côte Rôtie meets the test. It is no Rudyard Kipling in a bottle, making one suspect a defective memory or a defective cork.)

On days when I merely suspected money to be at the bank, I would continue from the Restaurant

des Beaux-Arts to the Boulevard des Italiens by
any variation of route that occurred to me, looking
in the windows of the rare-book dealers for the
sort of buy I could afford only once a month. Since
on most of my trips I drew a blank at the Crédit
Lyonnais, I had plenty of time for window-shop-
ping and for inspection of the bookstalls on the
quays. To this I attribute my possession of some
of the best books I own—the *Moyen de Parvenir,*
for example, printed at Chinon in the early seventeenth century, with the note on its title page:
"New edition, corrected of divers faults that
weren't there, and augmented by many others
entirely new."

On the *good* day, when I had actually received
the notification, I had to walk over again to collect,
but this time I had a different stride. Simply from
the way I carried myself when I left my hotel on
the Rue de l'Ecole de Médecine, my landlord, M.
Perès, knew that I would pay my bill that night,
together with the six or seven hundred francs I
invariably owed him for personal bites. He would
tap cheerfully on the glass of the window that
divided his well-heated office and living quarters
from the less well-heated entrance hall, and wave
an arm with the gesture that he had probably used
to pull his company out of the trenches for a
charge at Verdun. He was a *grand blessé* and a
Chevalier of the Legion of Honor, *à titre militaire,*
with a silver plate in his head that lessened his
resistance to liquor, as he frequently reminded
Madame when she bawled him out for drinking
too much. "One little glass, and you see how I am!"

he would say mournfully. In fact, he and I had usually had six each at the Taverne Soufflet, and he convived with other lodgers as well—notably with an Irishman named O'Hea, who worked in a bank, and a spendthrift Korean, who kept a girl.

At the restaurant, I would drink Côte Rôtie, as I had premeditated, and would have one or two Armagnacs after lunch. After that, I was all business in my trajectory across Paris, pausing only nine or ten times to look at the water in the river, and two or three more to look at girls. At the Crédit, I would be received with scornful solemnity, like a suitor for the hand of a miser's daughter. I was made to sit on a bare wooden bench with other wretches come to claim money from the bank, all feeling more like culprits by the minute. A French bank, by the somber intensity of its addiction to money, establishes an emotional claim on funds in transit. The client feels in the moral position of a wayward mother who has left her babe on a doorstep and later comes back to claim it from the foster parents, who now consider it their own. I would be given a metal check with a number on it, and just as I had begun to doze off from the effects of a good lunch, the Côte Rôtie, the brisk walk, and the poor ventilation, a *huissier* who had played Harpagon in repertoire at Angers would shake me by the shoulder. I would advance toward a grille behind which another Harpagon, in an alpaca coat, held the draft, confident that he could riddle my pretensions to the identity I professed. Sometimes, by the ferocity of his distrust, he made me doubt who I was. I would stand fumbling in the wrong pocket for my *carte d'identité*, which had a knack of passing from one part of my apparel to another, like a prestidigitator's coin, and then for my passport, which on such occasions was equally elusive. The sneer on Harpagon's cuttlefish bone of a face would grow triumphant, and I expected him to push a button behind his grille that would summon a squad of detectives. At last, I would find my fugitive credentials and present them, and he would hand over the draft. Then he would send me back to the bench, a *huissier* would present me with another number, and it all had to be done over again—this time with my Kafka impersonation enacted before another Harpagon, at another grille, who would hand out the substantive money. Finally, with two hundred times twenty-six francs, minus a few deductions for official stamps, I would step ou onto the Boulevard des Italiens—a once-a-month Monte Cristo. "Taxi!" I would cry. There was no need to walk back.

V

La Nautique

Mens *sana in corpore sano* is a contradiction in terms, the fantasy of a Mr. Have-your-cake-and-eat-it. No sane man can afford to dispense with debilitating pleasures; no ascetic can be considered reliably sane. Hitler was the archetype of the abstemious man. When the other krauts saw him drink water in the Beer Hall they should have known he was not to be trusted.

I, once, at fifty-two, committed myself voluntarily to a slimming prison in Switzerland, but I was suffering from only temporary insanity. I soon repented, but I stayed in because I had paid two weeks' nonboard in advance, and I didn't want to forfeit the fee, which was rather more than four meals a day would have cost me at Pierre's on the Place Gaillon, each with a half-bottle of Corton Charlemagne, another of La Mission Haut-Brion, and three healthful drinks of Calvados to follow.

It was like a mental hospital where, as a result of a mutiny, the inmates had taken over from the staff, and now addressed one another as "Doctor." All the kind, fat, sensible people like me, who longed for something decent to eat, were under restraining orders, while the *soi-disant* doctors, who were free to eat normally, chose to drink rosehip tea and eat muck made of apple cores and wheat germ. They permitted us to eat only minuscular quantities of that. The nurses and therapists ate in the same ironically denominated *Speise-sal*, and except that they had larger portions than we, appeared to slop in identical slop. (Once, as a special reward for fortitude, I got three peeled hazelnuts.)

The only sane man on the place, aside from us, was the masseur, a big Swiss named Sprüdli.

"And thou, eat thou this crap?" I asked him in my imperfect but idiomatic German.

"No," said Sprüdli, as he plucked my biceps like harp strings and let them snap. "I need my strength. I eat to home."

"And what has thou to home yesterday evening eaten?"

"*Blutwurst,*" he said, "and *Leberwurst.*"

I wished I hadn't asked, but masochism feeds on itself, especially when there is nothing else to eat. I had an appetite for self-inflicted pain that since then has helped me understand the submissiveness of prisoners in concentration camps.

"And what has thou to home yesterday evening drunk?"

"Wein," he said, *"und Bier."*

He wrenched one of my knees out of joint, then put it back in the socket with the gesture of a man making a massé shot at billiards.

Tears of hunger and pain filled my eyes.

Sprüdli was, after all, like the majority of Swiss, a German. Once he knew my hurt, he made a point of telling me at each visit his menu for the previous day.

"Good morning," he would say. "Calves' hocks have I yesterday at lunch to home eaten, with potato dumplings, and to dinner spring chicken with another time dumplings." Then he would laugh, even before I winced, because he was so sure I would. Good old *Schadenfreude*.

When I had served my time in this ruinously expensive para-Buchenwald, I set out for Pontarlier, on the French side of the border, where I had friends I had not seen since the war. To get there I had to change trains at Bern. By the time I reached that city I had the flu, and when I got through the customs barrier on the station platform at Pontarlier I tottered into France and fell into my friends' four arms. I still weighed quite a lot. They bore me home in the Peugeot and put me to bed, where I shivered under eight or nine blankets. I knew I would recover when I heard, as through a deep fog, the voice of that good Doubsien doctor, who reeked congenially of kirsch and pipe tobacco.

"But the man has been starved!" he said. "His constitution has been mined! You must give him to eat—but do not commence brutally; he could not support it. A guinea hen or two the first day, and some brook trout."

"And wine?" asked my angelic hostess. "He can have wine? He adores it."

"He mustn't exaggerate," Hippocrates said. "No more than two litres a day, and nothing heavy—perhaps a Mercurey. If his pulse is low, a little *marc d'Arbois*. No *fondues* until tomorrow. Then we can begin feeding him up!"

I left Pontarlier, like Mother after her reducing tours long ago, pounds heavier than when I flew to Zurich to get weight off. This episode has remained unique in my life: it is the only time I yielded to the temptation to give myself pain. I found others harder to resist.

In 1926, though, I had another route to keeping my weight within bounds. I liked to box, and I had an illusion that if I boxed a lot, I could eat and drink a great deal and even stay up late with the girls. The exercise would burn all that out. I was too young to know that if you do those three things often you will feel with increasing infrequency like boxing, and boxing is no fun unless you feel like it. This is because boxing makes you want to eat, but eating does not make you want to box. I had not yet heard the great Sam Langford say: "You can sweat out beer and you can sweat out whiskey, but you can't sweat out women." Sam had never had to contend with my toughest opponent of all, sheer gluttony.

At thirteen, when my Uncle Mike from San Francisco inducted me into the rudiments of the dulcet art, I was not a drinking man or a rake.

Later, at college and even in Providence, temptation had been sparse. On the *Journal* I worked a
night shift for forty dollars a week. That meant
I got a full sleep after work and ate plainly. Most
days I hit the YMCA gym about noon and sparred
a few rounds or jogged a couple of miles before
going into the newspaper office. I weighed between
160 and 170 pounds. In Paris my only exercise
was walking. For a while that was enough, and
then I began to feel guilty. Ralph Henry Barbour
and G. A. Henty were among the moralists in my
background; they had succeeded George Washington. The heroes of their screeds were constantly
in hard physical condition so they could play
left end or undertake dangerous missions behind
enemy lines. No overlay of Rabelais or Stendhal
could eradicate their depraved influence.

Uncle Mike, my mother's slightly younger
brother, was not one of the relatives who had
"done well." He had a pinched, Cruikshank kind
of face that had remained small while the jowl
grew and solidified around it, until it looked like
a small print in a large mat. The character he had
chosen for himself—the hot sport of 1900—like-
wise became set in the fat of respectability as he
settled down. He should have been a vaudeville
actor or a confidence man, but both his sisters had
married good providers, and he had formed the
bad habit of working for relations.

Mike was therefore a disappointment to his kin,
but he was an inspiring pedagogue. The academic
life might have suited him, now that I think of it,
but he had not pursued Minerva beyond the portals

85

of Lowell High School, preferring to scuttle down an alley in pursuit of burlesque girls. The object of boxing, Mike made clear from the first, was not self-defense. It was pleasure, like ocean swimming.

You do not go into the ocean to defend yourself from drowning. Indeed, the chances are slightly greater that you will drown if you go in than if you don't. Neither do you box to save yourself from getting a black eye.

The satisfactions outweigh the risks. Boxing is more social than swimming or poetry, because it is a dialogue. An infelicitous line invokes a disastrous rhyme.

I was an awkward child, fat from sitting still and reading, and had to learn all from the beginning, even to keeping my eyes open when popped on the nose. I talked learnedly about the names on the sports page, indeed, and when Mike asked me if I could box, I answered with assurance that I could. But I then stood up with my right hand forward and my feet close together. It was a moment of humiliation, but a good place to start from. I knew nothing at all. Mike taught me to stand, to move, to hit, always in the short line, but most important, the theme of boxing, which is, as in chess, annihilation.

Defense is either a preliminary to attack or an interlude between attacks. You move to beat the other fellow, not to avoid being beaten. Safety, relative though it be, lies in attack, too. You are safer inside a punch—which means inside its arc

86

—than stepping away from it, and possibly into its sweep.

More, if you are inside a punch you are in position to strike, but if you are outside it, you have merely escaped. This is the simple essence. Whatever other inferences may be drawn from it are optional and incidental.

Mike taught me, I am sure, less than he knew, but everything he gave me was right, or within good arguing distance thereof. To hunch the left shoulder over the jaw, for example, does not suit all styles, but he said it was Jim Jeffries' way. To half-rotate the arm while jabbing is considered by some purists an affectation, but Mike said it was Kid McCoy's corkscrew, and that made its appeal to me irresistible. He had the marks of California's Golden Age clear on his style. The Californians were like their contemporaries the Impressionists, graceful, direct, and full of light.

What charmed me more than anything was the craftily circumventional trick Mike taught me of catching the other fellow's best hand under your armpit and swinging him off balance, meanwhile punching away.

"Holding with one hand and hitting with the other is a foul," Mike explained, "but if the guy gets his glove caught under your armpit, how can you help it? And if you accidentally hit a guy in the mouth with the top of your head, bring your head up again to say you're sorry. If you are lucky you might catch him in the same place." This made me feel wise as well as brave.

My wisdom redounded to my disadvantage
once during that soft Paris year, when I was boxing with a young Mormon missionary at the American Baptist Center gym on the Rue Denfert-
Rochereau. We both had our heads down and
brought them up simultaneously. He must have
had another Uncle Mike. The right side of his head
hit the right side of mine. We split each other's
right eyelids, from brow to lash, neatly and iden-
tically. The blood ran as from two faucets; there
was no pain, but the mess was ridiculous. Amateur
first aid was hopeless. It would have posed a problem to a professional cut man like Whitey Bim-
stein. So we set out just as we were, in sweat shirts
and gym pants, and ran to a hospital on the Avenue de l'Observatoire, not far away. We left a
bloody trail as we jogged.

The Mormon was at the Sorbonne taking a
course in French culture so he could convert a
better class of people. He looked a real Joe College,
with slicked blond hair, but was a nice enough
kid. By now he must be a bishop.

We had a great reception at the hospital, where
nurses and interns found us *rigolo*—victims of
our passion for healthful exercise. There a resident closed the long vertical cut in my lid with
small metal clamps, which he put in with an
instrument like a stapler. It was too near the eye
for sutures, he said, and the stapler was quicker
and less painful. An old doctor at Cherbourg
took the last dressing off several weeks later and
left the clamps in. His theory was perhaps that
they would dissolve. The skin in time grew over

them, and the hair-thin white line, gravelly to the touch, is the nearest thing that I have to a dueling scar by which to remember my university days. It is also the nearest thing I have to a mining claim; grains of metal have continued through the years to work their way up to the surface, and I sometimes suspect that they breed or multiply by parturition.

My appearance when I returned to the Hotel Saint-Pierre kept M. Perès in laughs for a month.

That was the most animated episode of my athletic life in Paris. I had found the Center through a two-line ad in the Paris *Herald*. It had a small gymnasium with a basketball court and showers, but they were in use by French Baptist children most of the week. There may have been a school there as well as a church. I was not nosy.

For a minute fee, we non-Baptists were allowed to work out on Wednesday afternoons, and it was a bargain, because if you lived at a hotel you had to pay each time you took a bath. The weekly shower alone amortized your dues at the Center. Some of the odd lot who turned up made do with that one a week. Some played basketball or volley-ball, but I was the only Centrist keen on boxing. I owned the only gloves, and my efforts to proselyte were viewed with suspicion.

A few of the young painters and students were athletic, but putting on gloves intimidated them and they froze. There is no fun in boxing with a nonboxer: you feel silly hitting him, and then, when you let down, he catches you an awkward blow that hurts, and you have to say "Good man!"

when you want to murder him. I have read in numerous reminiscences since of the American Artists' Club, on the Boulevard Raspail, where literary figures like Hemingway and Morley Callaghan and Bob Coates beat each others' brains out constantly, but I never found that one. Raspail was far off my beat, and I don't suppose they would have boxed with anybody who hadn't published. The only American writer who used the Center was Joe Gollomb, a hairy, heavy-set, kindly man who ground out whodunits. He was thirty-eight, and I could not conceal my incredulity when he told me that he still had a sex life. There was also a thin, prim young man from Kansas named Harold Callender, who was a correspondent for *The New York Sunday Times Magazine*. He would not, I remember, take a drink, and would cause me embarrassment by sitting with us in a café and asking for a glass of water. When I last saw him, a few years ago, he was chief of the *Times* bureau in Paris and a reformed character. He bought me a splendid lunch and drank almost as much as I did.

When we had finished our moderate Wednesday exertions—mine grew more moderate by the week—three or four of us would walk together as far as the nearest café. Rue Denfert-Rochereau runs from the Lion de Belfort to a confluence with Avenue de l'Observatoire, which arrives almost instantly thereafter at the juncture of the Boulevards Montparnasse and Saint-Michel. (Avenue de l'Observatoire is, except for its name, a continuation of Saint-Michel—or Saint-Michel of Observatoire, if you start at the other end.) Denfert-Rochereau was an austere street with several convents, but no bars. So we had to walk to the junction of the boulevards for our drink, at the Closerie des Lilas. All of us had to walk that far together anyway, before our paths diverged.

By then it would be time for the *apéritif*, and we would all feel virtuous because we had performed the clean-life equivalent of attendance at mass. We had made our peace, for the week, with Ralph Henry Barbour.

We would knock off a couple of vermouths cassis, and then my acquaintances would turn off west along Montparnasse to join the other Americans, while I would turn down Saint-Michel alone, firm in my resolve to live the life of the French. I did not, of course, but I lived with them and among them, and among other assorted foreigners of the Quarter.

I liked the sensation of immersion in a foreign element, as if floating in a summer sea, only my face out of water, and a pleasant buzzing in my ears. I was often alone, but seldom lonely; I enjoyed the newspapers and books that were my usual companions at table, the exchanges with waiters, barmen, booksellers, street vendors, the old voices of the old professors in the lectures I irregularly attended, the sounds of the conversations of others around me, and finally, the talk of the girls I ended some evenings by picking up. This isolation dispensed me from defending my whims.

I was free to attend the operetta theaters, like

the Mogador and Gaîté-Lyrique, without fear of being called corny, or the Grand-Guignol without being reminded that it was *démodé*. One of the delights of Paris then was that several theatrical pasts coexisted with the present; one was not limited to a choice of contemporary or classic theater. Besides Romains and Giraudoux at the Théâtre des Champs-Elysées, and Molière and Racine at the State Theaters, there were constantly on tap the operettists of the early Third Republic, the bedroom farces and the Guignol of before the 1914 War, the classic clowns of the Cirque Medrano. Each had its public, and only segments of the public overlapped. That of the operettists consisted of nostalgics and provincials, proper old couples and their grandchildren come to celebrate their name-days. But seeing and hearing each of these theatrical modes for the first time and without preconception, I got the same lift out of *Les Cloches de Corneville*, let us say, as had Planquette's first audience in 1877, when it was as new as *No, No, Nanette* in 1927. The French circus burst on my vision as freshly as on that of Toulouse-Lautrec twenty-five years earlier. I was to recognize it later in the drawings that when I discovered the *cirque* I had not seen. The bedroom situations of the Théâtre du Palais-Royal struck me as of the utmost originality, and the surviving *chansonniers* in the manner of Aristide Bruant delighted me—I did not have the advantage of possessing friends *à la page* who could have told me they had gone out.

I remember the tender reverence with which I

heard Xavier Privas, the *Roi des Chansonniers,* a beautiful old man with a white spade beard, intone, at the tiny Théâtre des Noctambules in the Quarter:

"Pour qui sait aimer, les heures sont roses. . . ."

Pour qui savait some other infinitive, the hours were some other color. I forget what colors went with what particular hours, except for the *aimer-rose* link, but he ran through the spectrum: *penser, mourir, attendre; grises, blanches,* and perhaps *chartreuses.* I thought Privas had written the air as well as the lyrics, and it was not until long afterward that I learned it was the most hackneyed Brahms "Lullaby."

The Noctambules was a hall with a platform at one end and a bar at the other. It was in the Rue Champollion, an alley two blocks long bearing the name of the man who deciphered the Rosetta Stone. Champollion covertly paralleled the Boulevard Saint-Michel, sneaking like an assassin behind the Boul's back from the Rue des Facultés as far as the Rue Cujas, named for an illustrious jurist of the sixteenth century. The names of the streets of the Latin Quarter are designed to facilitate the acquisition of culture, like the noodles in alphabet soup. Gypsy's Bar, of which more hereafter, stood at the Cuja end of Champollion, and midway in the alley there was the Hotel Champollion, where the *séjours,* like an analyst's sessions, lasted fifty minutes, which permitted the couples to leave before they had to pay for another hour.

Besides Privas, the apostle of the noble and

pathetic, I heard at the Noctambules an old rascal named Georges Polin, who did a number in an ill-fitting French uniform of the red-pants era before 1914—the sort that must have looked so odd on the fastidious conscript Proust. Polin's material was drawn from Courteline, bespattered with latrine humor. His stage character was the clodhopping conscript, slyly stupid, lecherous, and confident, even after he had been had, that he had had the other fellow. It was clear that it was old, older than the red pantaloons of the costume. It had become so familiar to the great public that he could find no bookings in larger theaters, but like a *cassoulet* long on the stove, it was better than ever. Here, before the students who had never seen him in his glory, he was irresistible, like those potpourris of cuttings from silent film comedies that convulse present audiences. So I enjoyed not only what amused my Paris, but what had amused several earlier ones.

This living retrospective of the theater is something New York has never provided, except for films. The New York theater has always rejected the past, although with the slimmest imaginable justification, to judge from its output season by season. Paris was then a city of constant artistic innovation—of which I was unconscious, and if I hadn't been, would have been distrustful. But there was a past *concurrent* with the present. This is more nourishing than revivals, which tend to be arch and patronizing. Polin's bulbous red *trogne* with the pendulous upper lip and Privas' pretentious profile belong to the nineties, but I remember them as well as Maurice Chevalier and his wife of my era, Yvonne Vallée, framed in the spotlight of prime success at the Casino de Paris, singing "Leendy, Leendy, sweet as the shoogar can," and "Valentine." "Valentine," incidentally, is the ten thousandth version of *La Belle Heaulmière. "Elle avait,* etc." *Mais où sont les et cetera de 1926?*

In the affairs of the ring there was the same place reserved for age. Georges Carpentier was all through—you couldn't have got him a match in the United States in 1926-7 if you were Al Capone —but I saw him box an exhibition at the Salle Wagram with a mulatto named Jack Walker, and the exhibition topped a card of in-earnest bouts. From having seen him work the four rounds, without pressure, I can remember, and testify, that he had a fluent, beautiful style, with extremely fast reflexes—he seemed to be pouring into his man, like a curving stream, the blows winding around elbows and under arms and slipping like eels into the great breadbasket sea, then leaping like salmon across the dropped shoulder to the chin. I could see what he must have been when he still could take a punch. I have never thought since that the great American fighters he met before World War I carried him—he must have been a bit of a phenomenon, as a middleweight. Dempsey was a stream, too, but like a jet out of a fire hose, a straight-at-you flattener. I think Carpentier at his best would have been harder to elude although less instantly fatal. Of course he never was very big.

Walker, his foil at the Wagram, was a magnificently made light-heavyweight, who moved well in a style rather like Carpentier's—after all, the latter had set a fashion for the boxing generation that followed him. But Walker, I have heard since, lacked heart; he was a sparrer rather than a fighter.

The Carpentier style produced patterns that Dunoyer de Ségonzac caught in line drawings of a grace unequaled by any other draftsman of the ring. A hundred years after Thomas Rowlandson's "Cribb and Molyneux," Ségonzac made his fighters move like fighters. There was nobody in between. The lugs in "A Stag at Sharkey's" are just pushing. Bellows painted fights the way Jack London wrote about them. Thomas Eakins, though he did fine ring scenes, never showed his fighters in motion— one would be down, as in "Taking the Count," or both in their corners, or about to enter the ring.

The French style then coming in was the antithesis of Carpentier's—it was constricted, sly, and almost surly. The boxer, leaning slightly forward, walked in with elbows high and forward, the line from elbow to fist almost vertical. He conducted his operations from this cage, usually offering the top of his head as part of his defense. It was a style set, I believe, by an old-timer named Professor Fernand Cuny, who coached the French Olympic team. The new French fighters were beginning to come out of the amateurs instead of directly from the back alleys.

One of the toughest was Edouard Mascart, a knotty featherweight who on the night of January

25, 1927—a date I have verified from the *Ring Record Book*—took on Panama Al Brown at the Cirque d'Hiver, a building designed, as its name indicates, to house an indoor circus. It was high, because it featured aerial acts, and narrow, because real estate was valuable, and I remember that I climbed hundreds of meters of stairs to attain a height from which I looked down at the fighters' heads and shoulders. Brown was an oddity in more ways than one—he was five feet eleven inches tall and could make 112 pounds ringside. Withal he was a remarkably good boxer, one of those self-taught artists, like Kid Chocolate from Havana, who came out of the Caribbees letter perfect, as if they had, in one adolescence, invented for themselves all the developments of the last fifty years. He had first shown in New York in 1923 and gone almost three years without losing. He had then begun to take on heavier men, and good ones, and he lost several decisions. (There were rumors that in some of these bouts he was handcuffed by agreements he had to make in order to get work.) When he turned up in Paris he allowed his weight to rise to 118, and the extra six pounds endowed him with a punch like a welterweight. He was black, skinny, and had a long, pointed head. Two thirds of his length was legs, and he had long arms swinging from shoulders like a crossbeam. His torso was so narrow that his heart had standing room only. Mascart was ten pounds heavier and eight inches shorter.

It was not an epic battle. Mascart advanced behind the top of his head surrounded by the cage, but when he pulled a bar out of the cage to strike, Brown would insert a long left into the vacancy left by the displacement. Mascart would stagger back across the ring, amid the mad clamors of the crowd, astonished that he held his feet.

"*Il tient! Il tient!*" they chorused. "He stays, he resists!"

And "*Vas-y*, Mascart!"— "Hop to it."

He would put his head down and rush again, and this time Brown would pull him in with the left and uppercut with the right, lifting him off his feet. It was murder; Mascart might as well have been fighting a power mower with his face. The weight advantage, his lower center of gravity, and the constitution of an ox prolonged his suffering. It was one of the fanciest beatings I ever saw a man take, and the crowd, cheered throughout, not because he was winning, but because Brown didn't knock him out.

"*Il tient, il tient, il tient encore!*"

It was one of those situations that stay graven on the mind. Always now, when things are going wrong one after another, I rally myself with the cry "*Il tient!*"

In the fifth round *pouvait pas plus*—Brown hit him an uppercut that sedated him completely. When disaster starts throwing combinations, fortitude will not suffice. Yet, had Mascart held a moment longer, fate might have intervened. Hardly had the Frenchman subsided flat on his back when the admiring shouts changed to screams of vituperation against Brown. Everybody in the balconies threw something, and one *deus ex galleria* hit

Brown with an apple, right on the point of his head. Panama Al's seconds led him to his corner, as deep in dreams as his victim. The moral, I suppose, is: Never despair; perhaps God will throw an apple.

Had I had a companion in my wanderings, his reactions would have differed from mine and perhaps spoiled them. The matter of how much discomfort a man is prepared to undergo for an experience depends on how much it is worth to him. The best of friends can seldom agree on the price. (This is true even of a price in money.) Excursions are likely to become compromises, gratifying the full taste of neither. The man who pokes around alone may take a wrong turning at the junction of two streets and return from his ramble disappointed, but never recriminative. He has nobody to blame for his mistake. This is also a superiority of boxing over, say, bridge or football. There is no colleague to throw off on.

Granted that in later life a man will have to learn to get along with other people—I learn with horror that the knack is now taught in high school as a "social study"—that is all the more reason there should be a period in his life when he has to get along with nobody but himself. It will be a sweetness to remember.

I was not entirely a free particle in Paris, however, without touch with a French heart or *droite d'entrée* to a hearth. There was a family where I had the quality of an almost-relative. Monsieur and Madame, with their children, Suzette, seventeen, and Jean-Paul, fifteen, inhabited a vast apartment on the Avenue de la Motte-Picquet, near the Champ de Mars.

I had known them since my childhood, because they had lived near us on Long Island in what was then a fairly far-out but is now a very near-in suburb of New York. Monsieur had been sent to America before the 1914 War as sales manager for a great French silk mill. He had returned to fight, leaving Madame in what she considered straitened circumstances, and she had then given French lessons to the local ladies. My mother had been her star pupil. Suzette had gone to school with my sister. After the war Monsieur had returned, half-ill from the effects of gas. We had become friends, despite the difference in age. He was full of a suppressed Bohemianism, of the vintage of 1900. He looked like Don Quixote, as tall as de Gaulle, with a long drooping mustache *en grenadier*.

In 1925 he had been called back to France to a very good place in the old firm. For him America had been a place of Bithynian exile, but for Madame, to hear her talk after she got back, it had been a giddy whirl, an exotic paradise. Happiness, for her, was always some place where she used to be. One disaster, from Madame's point of view, was that they were again within the orbit of Monsieur's mother, who according to Madame had always favored his two brothers since Monsieur had married her. On the surface, though, all was smooth—the family was reunited, and, since Monsieur was prosperous, his mother could not bully him. Monsieur liked me because we had felt ourselves castaways in suburbia, and

Madame loved me as a visible symbol of that glorious world in which she convinced herself she had recently existed. As a matter of fact, she had been most unhappy there. It was through Monsieur that I joined La Société Nautique de la Marne, one of the two chief rowing clubs of the region. It was my last gesture of appeasement toward Ralph Henry Barbour and *Mens sana*.

The coach, a M. Parisot, was my direct sponsor, in spite of the fact I never saw him before I became a *sociétaire*. For years he had been chief clerk of an importing house in the Cité Bergère, one of the partners in which was one of the brothers of Monsieur. The brother, who first talked to Parisot about my *adhésion* to La Nautique, informed Monsieur, who informed me, that Parisot had been knocked in the eye at the prospect of having an American oarsman for the objective race of the season—against La Nautique's rival, the Rowing Club de la Seine.

Two years before, M. Parisot had witnessed the triumph of Yahlé, the American crew at the Olympics of 1924, and he expected to see a Yahlé type of oarsman when I reported at the clubhouse of La Nautique on the following Sunday. He was not completely disappointed in me. I wasn't as big as a varsity oarsman, but I was a lot bigger than most of the other *sociétaires*. His first deception, as he expressed it, came when I told him I had never rowed in my life, even in a skiff. He was of the opinion, however, that with application I would be able to figure in the debutant eight of the Nautique on the day of the great race and that in another summer I might be ripe for the senior boat. M. Parisot was a ruddy little man with a bristly black-and-gray mustache, a deep voice, and an air of command, which he had acquired in early life when he had been a coxswain. He was a Southerner, I believe, and on Sundays always wore a steamer cap pulled down over his eyes and a gray turtleneck sweater, to indicate the completeness of his release from sedate importing-office ways. M. Parisot, as *barreur*, which is French for cox, had once directed the unsuccessful activities of a French crew at Henley.

"It wasn't because of more savant manipulation of the oar that they beat us," he informed me on that first morning of our acquaintance, "but because of a superiority of brute force. They were horses, my lad."

The Société Nautique de la Marne had its seat at Joinville-le-Pont, which is a little suburban town that you reached from the Gare de Vincennes. The Société occupied an island in the Marne, accessible by a stairway from the stone bridge that gives Joinville-le-Pont its name. One of the first things I noticed about the Marne was that there did not seem to be much water in it. What water there was appeared to be full of long green weeds, and I wondered how I would ever be able to pull an oar through them. This problem turned out to have no importance.

Before inducting me into the mysteries of the sweep, M. Parisot said (I had sought him out as soon as I arrived on the island) it would be his pleasure to present me to my fellow *sociétaires* and, he hoped, my teammates of the future. When the presentations were finished it was time for dinner. I learned from a young man named Morin, to whom I had been presented, that the crews of the Société practiced only on Sundays when the weather was pleasant; there was consequently no time to waste on elaborate dinners. The *sociétaires* did not insist upon formalities, what the devil, one wasn't *chez* Foyot, what? So we had, as hors d'oeuvre, only a crock of duck *pâté*, a crock of *pâté* of hare, a few tins of sardines, muzzle of beef, radishes, and butter. Morin, who sat next to me, was almost abjectly apologetic. Two little girls in pigtails served the dinner. They were the daughters of the caretaker. He was not the best of caretakers, Morin said, but his wife, the little girls' mother, was an excellent cook. Morin was a handsome fellow and wore a royal-blue sweater with the arms knotted negligently around his neck even while he ate. The colors of the Société were blue and white. After the hors d'oeuvre we had a potato soup, then a *buisson de goujons*, a mound of tiny fried fish, for each of the *sociétaires*. After that, a leg of mutton with roast potatoes, a salad, cheese, and fruit. Red and white wine were there to take *à discrétion*, and most of the *sociétaires* had a brandy with their coffee as a digestive.

Naturally, one did not attempt violent exercise after such a meal. It would not be healthy, M. Parisot explained. A group of us took a stroll about the island. A *sociétaire* named Leclerc, the *chef de nage,* or stroke, of the senior eight, said that he didn't think he'd row that afternoon. "What the devil!" he said. "One works hard all week. Why sweat when you don't have to?"

We interrupted our walk to watch the shell of the Femina Sports, a women's athletic club which also went in for rowing. The shell was being towed upstream by a motorboat. The girls sat with their feet on the gunwales in order not to wet their slippers; their thighs were ravishing. I still remember the girl who sat at bow. She wore her hair, which was ash-blond, in a high mound on top of her head, and she had long earrings. When the girls got about a quarter of a mile above the island they decided not to row anyway, so the motorboat towed them back to their own float, a bit farther downstream. We of the Nautique were disappointed.

Toward half past four M. Parisot suggested that I essay the club's rowing machine. I planked myself down on the sliding seat. It was on a float on the side of the island away from Joinville. The motion of the float, it was explained to me, would partially accustom the beginner to the swell of the river. I seized the dummy sweep, and M. Parisot, pausing frequently lest I break into perspiration—the weather was as yet a trifle raw—began to impart to me that *savant* stroke of the oar which had discomfited the Rowing Club de la Seine on innumerable occasions. "Lengthen out," he adjured me. "Lengthen out. All the way back until you regard the types who pass on the bridge!"

Since the float was fairly close to the bridge, I had to lie back until my head almost touched the float in order to regard the pedestrians. This was at the bottom of my stroke. It is known technically, I learned afterward, as a long layback. I performed the *savant* stroke of the oar several times to M. Parisot's satisfaction. Then he began to notice an unusually long pause at the end of the layback. A girl was crossing the bridge who I thought looked as if she might be the bow oar of the Femina Sports. She was walking with a soldier from the school for army physical instructors at Joinville, and I could not help watching them.

M. Parisot decided I was tired. "Rest," he said. "It is sufficient for the first day."

On the next Sunday it rained. I telephoned to the clubhouse. One of the caretaker's little girls informed me that there would be no practice. "*Crotte!*" she said. "It isn't worth the trouble to come. It's a pity, because *Maman* had bought three fine suckling pigs."

The races, debutant and senior, against the Rowing Club de la Seine were to take place on July 14. It was only mid-April then, but I began to count the intervening Sundays: not more than twelve! Allowing for a certain amount of rain, we would have time for not more than ten practices, probably. According to American standards, I thought, this would be hardly enough. On the third Sunday I reported to the clubhouse early, in time for an *apéritif* before dinner.

"Today," M. Parisot said, "if you indicate sufficient progress, we launch you on the river. In a yawl for two—there's no place in the debutant eight, unfortunately. You will have Poirier as your comrade."

He presented Poirier. I can see him still—a pale, long-legged boy of about eighteen, with lank blond hair combed straight back. We shook hands like men about to embark on a desperate adventure. I wondered if Poirier could swim.

In turn we performed our exercises on the rowing machine for M. Parisot. He expressed himself as satisfied. The sky clouded over and a few drops of water fell.

"Attendez!" said M. Parisot. *"*You can take an *apéritif en attendant.*"

He held up a finger to the wind and looked dubiously at the Marne, which stretched at least ten yards from the island to the right bank. Fifteen minutes later, as Poirier and I sat in the clubhouse over two vermouths cassis, M. Parisot entered.

"The river is too turbulent, my boys," he said. "Another time, what the devil! Drownings, you know—that does a rowing club no good. Better luck the next time."

I rode back to Paris with Poirier in third class. Poirier was a nice fellow, an apprentice ironworker. At the Gare we had another vermouth cassis and parted with a promise to brave the Marne together next Sunday, come what might. The next Sunday it rained. The one after that was Easter and I wanted to spend it with friends in Neuilly. On the Sunday after Easter I suffered from *la gueule de bois*, which is French for hang-over. A week later I decided that it was no use going out to Joinville because I had probably lost my form. That was the end of the athletic phase of my *vie parisienne*.

VI

The Modest Threshold

In 1927, when I was on the Left Bank of the Seine learning to eat, Root, whom I did not then know, was champing his way through his own delightful and necessary apprenticeship on the opposite side of the river. (I use the verb "to eat" here to denote a selective activity, as opposed to the passive acceptance and regular renewal of nourishment, learned in infancy. An automobile receiving fuel at a filling station or an infant at the breast cannot be said to eat, nor can a number of people at any time in their lives.)

Root (we have since compared notes) was twenty-four—a year or so my senior—and was a copyreader on the Paris edition of the Chicago *Tribune,* a daily later merged with the New York *Herald Tribune's* Paris *Herald.* It astonished many that the Chicago *Tribune,* with its phobia about foreign entanglements, should maintain a Paris affiliate. The immortal Colonel Robert R. McCormick, the parent *Tribune's* publisher, had divided feelings about this himself, and he satisfied his conscience by keeping the Paris by-blow on the stingiest footing possible. Most of the American employees were stranded expatriates, who came cheap, because they were always in oversupply while prohibition lasted.

The future author of *The Food of France* was earning fifteen dollars a week, which then worked out to about four hundred francs—considerably less than the grant-in-aid I was receiving from my father for doing nothing, or next to it. Being obliged to work six nights a week, Root had less opportunity to spend money; because he was paid fortnightly, he had a maximum of one night every two weeks when he wasn't broke. The gastronomic secondary school that he attended was a small café kept by a couple named Gillotte in back of the printing plant that Colonel McCormick's least favorite child shared with a French newspaper.

The Gillottes offered the indispensable advantage of credit, which made up for a lack of variety in their menu. What there was was good, though, Root says now— "They would give you a good honest *gigot* with *haricots blancs* for almost nothing, which was what we could afford to pay." On his one flush night off, he would stop by the Gillottes' to pay his tab and have one on the house, but he would not stay to dine. He could afford more advanced instruction then. On the other nights, in the intervals between writing heads on cable stories, he would think of his menu for the magic evening, revising it five or six times, so that he had considerable pleasure even out of the dishes he decided not to order. So the bibliophile steals pleasure from a catalogue, the lover from his fantasies.

The cable news served up to Americans in Paris in 1927, as I remember it, consisted— apart from the inevitable sports results—of cheap shootings in Chicago, Jimmy Walker's didos in New York, and the grim, persistent efforts of the press to read humorous profundity into Calvin Coolidge's dim silence. Confinement with these items made Root understandably reckless; sometimes he and whatever colleagues were free on the one great night would venture higher than I ever dared—to Lapérouse, where, according to my bedside book, the *Guide du Gourmand à Paris* (1925 edition), the average price of a meal was thirty-five francs, or a dollar thirty-five.

The franc fluctuated, and the *Guide* was always a bit optimistic about the price you could get away for, even "without doing anything lavish." Actually, a meal at Lapérouse was likely to cost at least two dollars. For that I could get a slap-up dinner for myself *and* a girl at the Taverne Soufflet, on the Boulevard Saint-Michel. But since I had all my evenings free, I had to spread the money around.

Root's judgment is independent and frequently sound, but when he holds, in *The Food of France*, that Lapérouse is still out of the ordinary, I think it is a case of his memory's clouding his comprehension of the present. When I was there last, not even the *œufs en gelée* were a success; the yolks were hard, inside a casing of aspic without flavor, although a proper *œuf en gelée*, runny *à l'intérieur* and savory, is within the competence of any respectable charcutier. And the matelote of eels was not as good as you'd get in any Sunday fishermen's tavern along a riverside; in depressing fact, it was bad. There are certain simple and unavoidably cheap dishes that are the I-beams of French cookery and are not to be tampered with; wine and eels and bacon and onions and herbs and judgment go into a matelote, and the eels should be fresh. The wine can be as old as you please. Within these classic limits, as within the rules of a game, there are gradations of success, dependent on the quality and proportion of the ingredients and on the thermotactic gift, since no two stews reach their nearest approach to perfection in the same number of minutes—or, to be meticulous, of seconds. The good cook, like the good jockey, must have "a clock in his head."

Failure in rudimentary things is typical of large restaurants now, in France as well as here. The reason is the happy improvement in the human economic condition; it is harder every year to recruit boys of superior, or even of subnormal, intelligence for the long, hard, dirty apprenticeship, at nominal pay—or none, in the early years—that makes a cook. Nowadays, a boy is likely to spend those years in school and go directly into a factory or office job that pays better than the kitchen.

The apprentices became journeyman cooks, rising through the echelons. Without these, it is impossible to staff a large kitchen properly. A *saucier* now, if under forty, is likely to be a fellow who has learned, *en vitesse,* to make a few sauces. (If he is over forty and still a *saucier,* he is probably a drunk.) The fish cook who has learned as hastily and then practiced may be able to fillet a sole, but neither can do the other's work, or anyone else's, because neither is a rounded artisan, which is a necessary preliminary to bucking for artist. (There is a saying that, by exception, one is born a *rôtisseur,* but I should hate to entrust a guinea hen to a baby.) Nobody learns to boil an egg or watch a pot nowadays, because that isn't anybody's job in particular. Needless to say, none of these assembly-line cooks would ever be able to run a kitchen, but that is not yet the critical problem; the fellow at the top of the heap in a large French restaurant may even today be a great man, since the chances are that he started his apprenticeship forty years ago. But he cannot do all the cooking, and the effectiveness of supervision is limited by the capacity of those exposed to it. He is like a choreographer without executants, an Omar Bradley without officers of field or company grade.

In 1948, Gaston Magrin, then commodore-chef of the French Line and on the point of retirement, told me that if he were to open a restaurant it would have fifty seats at most, because that was the maximum number of clients one man could "responsibly" care for. Since then, the situation has deteriorated; there are even fewer experienced and

dependable *sous-chefs* to be had. The small restaurants where a talented owner and his wife have
direct control of the kitchen produce the best food
in France now, though in most cases it is far from
cheap. (The "good little holes where you eat well
for nothing" have vanished, like the stately restaurants where you ate superbly for a fortune.) In
such families, the proprietor is sometimes aided by
his progeny; the children have an inducement to
learn the profession the hard way, because they
hope to inherit a profitable business. The impetus
seldom lasts more than one generation, though;
the children never resist the temptation to expand
and spoil the joint.

Not all Root's nights of glory were spent in
spheres as exalted as Lapérouse; sometimes, he
tells me, he would dine in small restaurants that
are now defunct or that he can no longer find. The
small restaurant is evanescent. Sometimes it has
the life span of a man, sometimes of a fruit fly. In
these lost Atlantises, Root and his friends would
eat dinners ordered in advance and built around
some special discovery of the proprietor's, like a
haunch of illegally killed venison. (Poachers' cars
had powerful headlights, and the deer would stand
dazzled by the road.) "These feasts were rare occasions, and we always had to keep the price in
mind when we arranged them," Root wrote me not
long ago. "They bear out perfectly your theory that
the rich can be only dilettante eaters." (The eater's
apprenticeship, though less arduous, must be as
earnest as the cook's.) "But also, of course, the
nonfeast level was very high. Even at the present

expensive rates, though, it's pretty rare nowadays to have a memorable meal. I did have one pretty good one at the Relais Fleuri, in Rouen, not so long ago—all Norman. First that cream-of-mussel soup, then *canard au sang,* then what was about the best Pont-l'Evêque I ever encountered, finally a Norman soufflé, and after it a subtle Calvados. I had run into plenty of good strong Calvados before, but this was the first time I had come across one that could hold its own against a really top-notch brandy."

The letter indicates that Root, at sixty or so, has not yet fallen completely for the hepatic fallacy, or obsession with the liver, which has taken so much of the fun out of French life. His note on the Calvados is the most encouraging bit of news I have heard from that country in years. Evidently the casks that the British Army overlooked are be-ginning to mature. (The Americans, in their zone of Normandy, left none.) Root's notion that Cal-vados, at its best, is not better than brandy, how-ever, is an indication only of the truth that no one man can be expected to know everything. Like the Norman, Calvados matures slowly and pays no taxes, but it is full of craft; brandies are precocious and superficial by comparison. As for the soufflé, I should have omitted it and preceded the rest of the meal with a dozen Norman oysters. I should also perhaps have introduced a bit of turbot (not more than a pound) between the mussel soup and the duck, to bring myself more gradually up the evolutionary scale—mollusks, fish, bird. In a menu so unpretentious, the cheese must represent the

world of mammals from which it is a derivative.
Root's weakness for soufflés, I suspect, traces
back to the soda fountains of Fall River, but despite this sentimental lapse—like the *lapsus lapérouse*—Root is no indiscriminately indulgent lip-
smacker. For example, he attacks the touted cuisine of Lyons as sharply as G. G. Coulton having
a crack at a Catholic medievalist:

My personal experience has been never to
have eaten a really good meal in Lyons [he
writes in his book, insuring an auto-da-fé if he
ever goes there under his own name]. Lyons is
a heavily bourgeois city . . . which has always
vaguely reminded me of Philadelphia . . .
[and] the cooking of Lyons fits the character of
the city—it is hearty rather than graceful, and
is apt to leave you with an overstuffed feeling.
[It may be seen by his Rouen menu, however,
that Root does not stuff too easily.] The cooking
of Burgundy is hearty, too, but there is a livelier
imagination connected with it. This is not to
say that Lyonnaise cooking is not good of its
kind, but its kind is not spirited. . . . One of
the commonest dishes associated with the city's
name—*pommes lyonnaises*—means simply
German-fried potatoes cooked with onion.
. . . When Lyonnaise cooks set out to be elaborate, they produce rich, liver-assaulting dishes
[this is the first known instance of Root's ac-
knowledging that he has a liver], even with such
a simple start as chicken—for instance, *poul-
arde demi-deuil*, fowl in half mourning, in
which the bird is accompanied by sweetbreads
of lamb and slices of truffles cooked in Madeira.

. . . Considering the heaviness of the cooking of Lyons, it seems somewhat astonishing that the Pyramide, at Vienne, so nearby . . . manages to get so much subtlety into its cooking. Even so, the local tradition of richness remains. When the Pyramide attacks trout, possibly the most delicately flavored of all fish, it stuffs it and then braises it in port wine—a triumph, but of the Lucullan rather than the purist school, which takes its trout *au bleu*—very fresh and boiled, with no adornment to detract from the basic flavor of the fish itself. Finally, the conclusion of a Pyramide meal, with all the surrounding tables covered with trays of tempting little cakes and pastries of every imaginable variety, is calculated to send the diner away some pounds heavier than when he came.

Root admires La Pyramide, on the whole, but he holds that no restaurant on a byway can be called truly great, since its clients come a long way to eat its specialties and it need scarcely ever change its menu. The truly great restaurateur is the one who can please essentially the same clientele week after week without boring or disappointing it. *La cuisine française* is not one cuisine but a score, regional in origin, shading off into one another at their borders and all pulled together at Paris. Since certain of these cuisines are almost antithetical to certain others, the self-styled lover of *la cuisine française* without qualification is simply admitting that he has no taste at all. He is like the French majors at American colleges; in order to get all A's, in one year they profess a profound admiration for Racine and in another for Stendhal, who found Racine an inexpressible bore. (The worst offenders in this branch of conformity, though, are *lycéens* in France, who, to obtain the grades on which their future careers largely depend, swallow whole the glories of every writer celebrated in a rigid curriculum. The savagery with which French scholars turn upon their predecessors in their own specialty is a direct result of the exaggerated subservience demanded on the way up.)

It is possible, of course, to like something in the cuisine of any province—or, rather, nearly impossible not to. Any sensitive eater, though, must prefer the essential line of some regional cuisines to that of others. I agree with Root that Dijon, for example, seems to have no bad restaurants and that the good Burgundian cook "achieves . . . a trumpeting perfection." This good man, or woman, Root says, "does not take a delicate trifle and, by the subtle application of refined seasonings, transfigure it with an ethereal sauce into a whispering perfection." (He here defines a kind of cooking for which he and I have a limited regard.) Burgundian food, he says, "is the *cuisine bourgeoise* at its best, or peasant cooking elevated to its greatest possible heights. It is often said that you need a solid stomach to live on Burgundian cooking, but Burgundian cooking develops solid stomachs."

And yet Dijon and Lyons are little more than a hundred miles apart—a safe distance between sound and unsound cultures in the Middle Ages but an insufficient barrier against contamination since the coming of the motorcar.

Thirty-five years ago, at Mâcon—a third of the way north from Lyons to Nuits-Saint-Georges, which is where I place Burgundy's heart—I had an alarming experience of the encroachment of the Lyonnais. The proprietor of the small city's leading hotel was a magnificent figure of a man who wore a chef's toque two feet high. (It was in those times a favorable sign when a hotel owner wore cook's garb; the beds might prove hard, but the food would be good. Lately, it seems to me, all hotel owners dress that way—it is a come-on.) Monsieur B. was sincerely a cook, but the axis of his culinary eye had shifted until he saw the main body of dinner as a perfunctory hors d'oeuvre to the sweets. His preliminary menu—consommé with shredded carrots, sole slicked with sauce (and this in a town by a river full of humbler, tastier fish), and, finally, veal *glacé*—reminded me depressingly of the Hamburg-American Line. Then squads of assistants, also in toques, would begin to roll in trolleys of pastry and confectionery —*vacherins, suissesses, mille-feuilles, meringues, îles-flottantes de Tante Marie*, and hundreds of sugary kickshaws I was unable to identify. Monsieur B. personally plied me with these, in the manner of a soprano volunteering unsolicited encores. I, at twenty-three, had not the nerve to turn him down; it was the first time I felt sick on *la cuisine française*. After this honeyed surfeit, at which I displayed hypocritical delight, the patron imposed himself upon me while I had a drink on the house.(He was astonished that I preferred cognac to Bénédictine or Cointreau.) "It is not in this little region that one could learn to cook so," he said with complacency. (I sadly thought that there was probably not a woman in town who couldn't cook more to my taste.) "I retired here and bought this hotel at the beginning of the war. Until then, for twenty years, from the time I left Lyons as a young *chef pâtissier*, I was chief cook for *le Kaiser Guillaume II*." In the years since, this somber episode has helped me define what I don't like about *la cuisine lyonnaise*.

The dinner at Mâcon peculiarly distressed me because it was one of my constantly fewer chances to further my education before leaving France, and it was wasted. The academic year at the Sorbonne was over, and I was in full retreat from Paris to Providence, via Marseille, where I was to embark on the *Patria*, of the Fabre Line. I had chosen Marseille as a port of departure because it would give me an excuse to eat and drink my way through Burgundy en route—or at least to nibble and gulp at a small part of its glory. My father, a grim chancellor now, had cut the fiscal supply line, and I had arranged by letter to resume my old employment at the Providence *Journal*, at the increased salary of sixty dollars a week. This would not have been a bad prospect to look forward to, if I had not been quitting one so much more splendid.

I descended from the Paris-Marseille express at Dijon to eat the first rear-guard action of my anabasis. There was one advantage in my position: I had more than sufficient money for the limited time left to me. I could afford some good bottles. At the Restaurant Racouchot, in the Place d'Armes, at Dijon, I made the acquaintance of *caille vendangeuse* and drank a bottle of Corton Clos du Roi. Having demonstrated my taste for the beautiful, I asked the waiter to recommend a small inn among the vineyards, where I might eat and drink well between long walks, or take long walks between heavy meals. Pedestrianism was always my balance for voracity; they were countervailing joys. Walking, I consumed what I had eaten, built up appetite for more, had noble thoughts, and spotted likely-looking restaurants.

The waiter recommended the Auberge de l'Etoile, at Gevrey-Chambertin, a village of blessed associations. At the Auberge, I fell in with the greatest host of my life—a retired second lieutenant *de carrière* named Robaine, who had risen from the ranks in the course of thirty years in the colonial Army. Robaine took me to all the cellars of the commune and the communes adjoining, representing me as a rich American bootlegger come to the Côte d'Or, the Golden Slope of Burgundy, to buy wine for the cargo of a fabulous *bateau-cave*—a wine-cellar ship that would be sailed into New York Harbor and hoisted by night ("like a lifeboat but on a huge scale, understand?") into a skyscraper with a specially prepared false front. In that way, I got to drink more good wine than most men are able to pay for in their lives, and

Robaine drank along with me—"pushing" the merchandise as he drank, and winking grossly at the proprietors of the vineyards, to indicate that he was conspiring with *them* to get a good price from *me*. At night, I would stagger home to eat the *jambon persillé*—parsley-flavored ham with mustard and pickles—that every meal began with, followed by hare or beef or fowl in a sauce of better wine than you could buy in other regions in labeled bottles. All the good wine I could drink came with the meals, but Robaine had invented the bootlegger story to get at the superlative wine of the vineyardists. He was a Lorrainer, from Nancy or Metz, and so an outsider, possessing no vineyards of his own.

One day, I varied the hospitality of the *cavistes* of Gevrey-Chambertin, Fixin, and Vougeot, the nearest communes, with a pedestrian expedition to Nuits-Saint-Georges, six miles away. There, in the restaurant of one of the two local hotels, I sat at the common table, where I was soon joined by a young man of my own age—a scholarly chap interested in foreigners—who said that he was bookkeeper-manager for a local wine merchant. Presently, he asked me how I liked the wine I had before me. The wine was a superb bottle of Grands-Echézeaux, but with a presence of mind learned from Robaine, I said that while it was good, it had limitations. Prodded, I even confessed to a trifle of disappointment. I said I had drunk as good bottles of Burgundy in Paris, even in Ireland; one expected that when one came to the birthplace of wine and asked the proprietress to furnish her best bottle . . . It was one of the most mendacious moments of my life.

The young Frenchman, appalled, said that he would speak to Madame. I begged him not to. He bit his lip. Finally, he said, "I cannot tolerate that you should carry away such a mediocre impression of our cellars. I invite you to sample what we call good wines at *our* place." Looking at the label on my now empty bottle—which was fortunately not that of his firm—he whispered, "Between you and me, the fellow who bottled that, although he is my boss's cousin, is a sharp chap. Doubtful integrity." After that, of course, he had to start me off on something that he considered better than the wine I had downed.

The afternoon I spent in the cellars of his firm was one of the happiest of my life. I regret that I have forgotten the firm's name. I was lucky to remember my own. After sipping the first glass he poured for me, I said, "It certainly beats the other for velvet, but the Echézeaux had a certain vigor, all the same, that is not to be despised." The next, I conceded, had an eternally youthful masculinity —but the Echézeaux, much as I had depreciated it, had had a certain originality. When I had drunk myself as tight as a New Year's Eve balloon, I admitted that the last wine he offered was indeed clearly superior to the bottle at the hotel. This was polite, but a lie. "*That*," I said, "is what I call Burgundy." It was a Romanée-Conti of some sort, and first-rate. "Well worth a voyage from North America to taste. Thunderously superior to that stuff I had with lunch." My benefactor was pale with gratitude. But the bottle at the hotel had been the best of the day.

That short week, thirty-five years ago, was my true initiation into the drinking of Burgundy. My introduction to the wine at its best and in profusion can only be compared to the experience of a young woman I know who, having attended progressive schools all the way to college, had her first massive introduction to Shakespeare *and* the Old Testament in the same year. My introduction was a bit overwhelming, but I had had a stout preparation for it during the academic year at the Sorbonne, when I passed my oenological novitiate experimenting among the Tavels and Côte Rôties of the Restaurant des Beaux-Arts. Drinking Richebourg without this training would have been like a debutant prizefighter's meeting Archie Moore in a feature bout; he would not be up to it and would never know what hit him. Burgundy has the advantage—to which a young palate is particularly sensitive—of a clear, direct appeal, immediately pleasing and easy to comprehend on a primary level. This is a quality compatible with greatness. Shakespeare and Tolstoy, because more accessible, are not necessarily inferior to, say, Donne and Dostoevski. The merits of the Parthenon sculptors are not inferior to those of the primitives for being easier to recognize. Burgundy thus has two publics: one (which it shares with Bordeaux) that likes it for its profound as well as its superficial qualities, and one that likes it only because it is easy to like. This second public

is its monopoly, and has increased vastly since the
Second World War, with the wide dissemination
of money among Frenchmen unused to affluence,
and the new tourism, spurred by the airlines in
both Britain and America, that is made up of people whose holidays were never before long enough
to allow them to penetrate the Continent. The double public has, in my view, made Burgundies double the price of equally good clarets—a condition
clearly reflected in the prices of wines exported to
America. (That is, if you like both clarets and Burgundies, you can do as well with two dollars in-
vested in a bottle of claret as with four dollars in-
vested in Burgundy.*)

In Paris itself, Burgundies are so far out of
sight that even expensive restaurants feature pe-
ripheral and approximative growths—some good,
some merely not bad, and nearly all claiming a
relationship to "the Beaujolais." (If the Beaujolais
region were to produce all the wines, bottled and
en carafe, that are sold in its name, it would have
to be larger than Alaska. One reason the French
held on to Algeria so stubbornly was that with its
loss three-quarters of "the Beaujolais" would disappear.) The essentials of these wines are a
"fruity" taste and a liberal degree of alcohol.

And yet Burgundy is a lovely thing when you
can get anybody to buy it for you. Root, I think, is
still a Burgundy man. "Bordeaux," he writes, "from
the ancient city of Romans—inheritor of the sophisticated Latin tradition—is grown in the region

* The disparity is less now (late 1962) than when this
was first written, but, I think, still exists.—A.J.L.

of a great port which has known an urban and cosmopolitan civilization for centuries; it is suave, polished, civilized. Burgundy, from the region of the swashbuckling Grand Dukes of the West, the lusty sons of inland soil, grown where men lived close to the land, remained rustic in richness, and exerted their own influence outward more readily than they welcomed other influences directed inward, is full-bodied, strong, earthy."

It is much easier to prove a relation between the chemical composition of the soil and the kind of wine it produces, though, than between the nature of the wine and the local civilization. Hymettus, for example, which grows on a mountain overlooking Athens, has no hint of philosophy or ancient civilization in it. The best wine grown near Rome is no great shakes, either; the marble in the soil that was grand for sculpture is not much good for the vine. As for the vintages of Lebanon, which was Phoenicia, and of Egypt, the cradle of the oldest civilization, they are less suave and polished than wine grown on the islands of Lake Erie.

In Marseille, waiting for my ship to sail, I paddled about in bouillabaisse. The *Patria* was of Marseille, the owners were Marseillais, and the officers were Corsicans, with the exception of the doctor, who did fine needlework. The crew on deck were Italianate Frenchmen from the Old Port, and the stokers were Senegalese. She was a delightful Conrad kind of ship that took the dull certainty out of peacetime sea travel. (Eventually, she exploded and capsized in Haifa, killing scores of homeless Jews who had been refused admission to Pales-

tine.) Providence was to be her first port of call in
the United States, and she went by way of Genoa,
Naples, Palermo, Madeira, and the Azores—nine-
teen days. This was the direct express route; other
Fabre liners had more circuitous itineraries. When
I got back to Providence, I was met by a fellow
worker on the *Journal*, who helped me smuggle
five bottles of champagne and several of cognac
past the customs men and prohibition agents. I
knew I was home again.

Root, meanwhile, remained in Paris, where I
had not known he was. He ate assiduously and
judiciously, improving his circumstances after the
Paris edition of the Chicago *Tribune* folded and
left him free to earn a living. When I returned,
early in October of 1939, both our situations were
different, and so was that of Paris. A war, such as
it was, had begun, and both of us were correspondents—he for a tabloid known as the Chicago
Times, a Copenhagen newspaper, and the Mutual
Broadcasting System, concurrently. At that stage
it was such an equivocal war, and had so limited
an interest for neutrals, that none of Root's em-
ployers thought it justified sending a full-time
representative. Root was what newspapers call a
stringer.

The war's touch on Paris was so light that
the government continually organized tours of the
front for French *littérateurs en vue,* in the course
of which a conducting officer would show them
the Germans and remind them that although few
shots were being fired—and those through nerv-
ousness or inadvertence—both antagonists were

armed. Returning to the Berkeley Restaurant or the Pavillon de l'Elysée, the men of letters would assure their colleagues that there was a war, and then, in long articles in the dozen or so popular newspapers, tell the readers of the emotions they had experienced in the contemplation of what might happen. The government was less eager to send neutral correspondents on such tours; they might not have been so easily impressed. It kept most foreign correspondents hanging about Paris, allowing only a few at a time to go up and see the sights—a selected portion of the impregnable Maginot Line, the Rhine bridge at Kehl, and the like. It was the most gradual introduction to warfare imaginable, and when, in the following May, the war became *de facto*, we were as unprepared for it as the poor old generals and their bored troops. The correspondents who had succeeded in staying on edge through the intervening months —the prophets of doom—were justified, but it had required effort or a built-in neurosis.

When I arrived in Paris, I was excited and apprehensive, and determined, if I got the chance, to sell my life dearly at my French friends' side. I had the scene by heart in fantasy: I would snatch up the rifle dropped by a falling *tirailleur* and die lying on my belly on a ridge, in the manner of Robert Jordan in *For Whom the Bell Tolls*, meanwhile snuffing out Huns like candle flames in a shooting gallery (where I had practiced several times before embarking). It is an image of his own demise that often occurs to the writer militant; Mathieu, in Sartre's long novel *La Mort dans*

l'Ame, does it that way, firing from a belfry. But
after several months of *attente* in a near-normal
Paris, unbombed and unexcited, I began to hope
that the whole thing would blow over, leaving me
with the glory of having covered a war and none
of the inconveniences possibly to be anticipated.

During this doldrum period, I met Root for the
first time; it was at a weekly luncheon meeting of
the Anglo-American Press Association of Paris, at
the Restaurant Drouant, which has good oysters.
Soon he became a familiar; we had a passion in
common. His face in those days was the precise
color of the inside of a *châteaubriant* that is between rare and medium rare. His firm and broad-
based jaw appeared to be an ideal instrument of
mastication, but his rounded chin and friendly
eyes announced a man readier to crunch a lark's
carcass than tear a tiger's throat. A kindly and
humorous man of wide and disparate interests, he
could talk well of many things, but our conversations, from the day I met him, were preponder-
antly about what we had eaten, or were about to
eat, or wished to eat—a topic varied by discus-
sions of what we had drunk or would like to drink
with it.

I could now afford to eat wherever I cared to.
During my American interim, my appetite had
been sharpened; now, returned to Paris, I was
ready to fly with the wings of larks, pheasants, and
woodcock. I took up quarters at the Hôtel Louvois,
on the little square that faces the Rue de Richelieu,
thus abandoning the quarter haunted by Villon in
favor of one that is sacred to the memory of Sten-

dhal. Villon, although there are no contemporary portraits of him, is conventionally represented by illustrators as he described himself: "Lean, sunken cheeks, starved belly." His passion for good food was a fixation on the unattainable, like Rudel's for La Princesse Lointaine, or Chartier's for La Belle Dame Sans Merci. Stendhal, however, enjoyed having his picture painted and left many likenesses. They all agree in the convexity of his front elevation—a magnificent background for a watch chain, an advantageous stuffing for a brocaded waistcoat. The difference in the profiles of the resident ghosts symbolized the gastronomic disparity between their respective neighborhoods. The Square Louvois was surrounded by fine restaurants.

In the twenties, the Rue Sainte-Anne, a narrow street running from near the Théâtre Français end of the Avenue de l'Opéra to the Rue Saint-Augustin and skirting the Square Louvois *en passant*, had been rendered illustrious by a man named Maillabuau, a gifted restaurateur but a losing horseplayer who had no money to squander on décor. He turned his worn tablecloths into an asset by telling his customers that he wasted none of their contributions on frills—all went into the supreme quality of his materials and wines. A place with doormen in uniforms, he would say—a place with deep carpets and perhaps (here a note of horror would enter his voice) an orchestra—was *ipso facto* and *prima facie* a snare. He would then charge twice as much as any other restaurant in Paris. My memories of visits to Maillabuau's—

visits that I had enjoyed only by stratagem—were so pleasant that I had chosen the Hôtel Louvois in order to be near it.

All during my year at the Sorbonne, the *Guide du Gourmand à Paris* had served as the Baedeker for my exploratory splurges when I had money enough to try restaurants off my usual beat. The author addressed his book to the gourmand, rather than to the gourmet, he said, because it was impossible to like food if you did not like a lot of it; "gourmet" was therefore a snob word, and a silly one. This predisposed me in his favor. But it was his subject matter that held me captive. The restaurants were categorized as "of great luxury," "middling-priced," "reasonable," and "simple," but all were warranted "good," and there were about a hundred and twenty-five of them. At the head of the "luxury" group was a "first platoon" of six restaurants (of which today only one survives, and that scarcely worthy of mention). Maillabuau, despite the worn tablecloths, figured among the ten others in the "luxury" group. In my own forays, "reasonable" was my ceiling, but I liked to read about the others—those financially unattainable Princesses Lointaines. I knew the description of Maillabuau's by heart:

Sombre, almost lugubrious front. If the passerby is not warned, never will he suspect that behind that façade, having crossed that modest threshold, he can know the pure joys of gastronomy! How to know, if one is not a gourmand, that here the sole is divine, that the *entrecôte Bercy* has singular merits, that the

pâté of venison is beyond equal, that the burgundies (especially the Chambertin) are of the
year that they should be, and that the *marc*
resembles embalmed gold? How to know that
only here, in all Paris, are made ready the fat
squab guinea-hens anointed with all the scents
of the Midi? Staggering bill, which one never
regrets paying.

I had no thought of crossing that modest threshold myself until one warm morning in the late
spring of 1927, when it occurred to me that my
father, mother, and sister would be arriving in
Paris in a few weeks—they were waiting only for
the beginning of the summer holiday at the Connecticut College for Women, where my sister was
now a sophomore—and that in the natural course
of events they would ask me, the local expert,
where to dine. My mother and sister favored the
kind of restaurant where they saw pretty dresses
and where the *plat du jour* was likely to be called
"Le Chicken Pie à l'Américaine," but my father
had always been a booster for low overhead and
quality merchandise; they were the principles that
had guided his career as a furrier. Russian sable
and ermine—with baum or stone marten if a
woman couldn't afford anything better—had always been his idea of decent wear. His views on
fur were a little like J. P. Morgan's on yachts—
people who had to worry about the cost shouldn't
have them. Foxes began and ended, for him, with
natural blacks and natural silvers; the notion of a
fox bred to specifications would have filled him
with horror. Seal had to be Alaskan seal, not what

was called Hudson seal, which meant muskrat.
Persian lamb had to be *unborn* Persian lamb, not
mutton.

As I had anticipated, when my family arrived
in Paris they did indeed consult me about the
scene of our first dinner together. So Maillabuau's
it was. When we arrived before the somber, almost
lugubrious front, my mother wanted to turn back.
It looked like a store front, except for a bit of scrim
behind the plate glass, through which the light
from within filtered without éclat.

"Are you sure this is the right place?" she asked.

"It's one of the best restaurants in the world," I
said, as if I ate there every day.

My father was already captivated. "Don't give
you a lot of hoopla and ooh-la-la," he said, with approval. "I'll bet there are no Americans here."

We crossed the modest threshold. The interior
was only half a jump from sordid, and there were
perhaps fifteen tables. Old Maillabuau, rubicund
and seedy, approached us, and I could sense that
my mother was about to object to any table he proposed; she wanted some place like Fouquet's (not
in the *Guide du Gourmand*). But between her and
Maillabuau I interposed a barrage of French that
neither she nor my sister could possibly penetrate,
though each chirped a few tentative notes. "I have
brought my family here because I have been informed it is the most illustrious house of Paris,"
I told him, and, throwing in a colloquialism I had
learned in Rennes, a city a hundred years behind
the times, I added, "We desire to knock the bell."

On hearing me, old Maillabuau, who may have

thought for a moment that we were there by mistake and were about to order waffles, flashed a smile of avaricious relief. Father, meanwhile, regarding the convives of both sexes seated at the tables, was already convinced. The men, for the most part, showed tremendous *devantures*, which they balanced on their knees with difficulty as they ate, their wattles waving bravely with each bite. The women were shaped like demijohns and decanters, and they drank wine from glasses that must have reminded Father happily of beer schooners on the Bowery in 1890. "I don't see a single American," he said. He was a patriotic man at home, but he was convinced that in Paris the presence of Americans was a sign of a bunco joint.

"Monsieur my father is the richest man in Baltimore," I told Maillabuau, by way of encouragement. Father had nothing to do with Baltimore, but I figured that if I said New York, Maillabuau might not believe me. Maillabuau beamed and Father beamed back. His enthusiasms were rare but sudden, and this man—without suavity, without a tuxedo, who spoke no English, and whose customers were so patently overfed—appeared to him an honest merchant. Maillabuau showed us to a table; the cloth was diaphanous from wear except in the spots where it had been darned.

A split-second *refroidissement* occurred when I asked for the *carte du jour*.

"There is none," Maillabuau said. "You will eat what I tell you. Tonight, I propose a soup, trout *grenobloise*, and *poulet* Henri IV—simple but exquisite. The classic *cuisine française*—nothing complicated but all of the best."

When I translated this to Father, he was in complete agreement. "Plain food," he said. "No *schmier*." I think that at bottom he agreed that the customer is sure to be wrong if left to his own devices. How often had the wives of personal friends come to him for a fur coat at the wholesale price, and declined his advice of an Alaskan seal —something that would last them for twenty years—in favor of some faddish fur that would show wear in six!

The simplicity of the menu disappointed me; I asked Maillabuau about the *pintadou,* fat and anointed with fragrance. "Tomorrow," he said, posing it as a condition that we eat his selection first. Mother's upper lip quivered, for she was *très gourmande* of cream sauces, but she had no valid argument against the great man's proposal, since one of the purposes of her annual trips to Europe was to lose weight at a spa. On the subject of wines, M. Maillabuau and I agreed better: the best in the cellar would do—a Montrachet to begin with, a Chambertin with the fowl.

It was indeed the best soup—a simple *garbure* of vegetables—imaginable, the best trout possible, and the best boiled fowl of which one could conceive. The simple line of the meal brought out the glories of the wine, and the wine brought out the grandeur in my father's soul. Presented with one of the most stupendous checks in history, he paid with gratitude, and said that he was going to take at least one meal a day *chez* Maillabuau during the rest of his stay. The dessert, served as a concession to my sister, was an *omelette au kirsch*, and Maillabuau stood us treat to the *marc*, like embalmed gold. Or at least he said he did; since only the total appeared on the check, we had to take his word for it. The *omelette au kirsch* was the sole dessert he ever permitted to be served, he said. He was against sweets on principle, since they were "not French," but the *omelette* was light and healthy. It contained about two dozen eggs.

The next day we had the *pintadou*, the day after that a *pièce de bœuf du Charolais* so remarkable that I never eat a steak without thinking how far short it falls. And never were the checks less than "staggering," and never did my father complain. Those meals constituted a high spot in my gastronomic life, but before long my mother and sister mutinied. They wanted a restaurant where they could see some dresses and eat *meringues glacées* and *homard au porto*.

So in 1939, on my first evening in wartime Paris, I went straight from the Louvois to the Rue Sainte-Anne. The Restaurant Maillabuau had vanished. I did not remember the street number, so I walked the whole length of the Rue Sainte-Anne twice to make sure. But there was no Maillabuau; the horses at Longchamp had eaten him.

VII

The Afterglow

When I returned to Paris in the fall of 1939, after an absence of twelve years, I noticed a decline in the serious quality of restaurants that could not be blamed on a war then one month old. The decline, I later learned, had been going on even in the twenties, when I made my first studies in eating, but I had had no standard of comparison then; what I had taken for a Golden Age was in fact Late Silver. Like me, Root, when he made his first soundings in the subject in 1927, was unaware that the watershed was behind us and that we were on a long, historic downslope. Enough of the glory remained to furnish us with memories by which to judge the punier times ahead, though; the food of France in 1926-27 still constituted the greatest corpus of culinary thought

and practice anywhere. The only touted challenger
for the lead then was China, and the only touts
were people who wanted to let you know they had
been there. When you got these Orientalized *fines
gueules* to a table where they had to use a knife
and fork instead of chopsticks, they could not
tell the difference between a Western sandwich
and a *darne de saumon froid sauce verte*. In most
cases, their sole preparation for gourmandizing
had been a diet of institutional macaroni in a Mid-
western seminary for medical missionaries, and
any pasture the Lord led them to was bound to be
better.

Chinese *haute cuisine* is unlikely to improve under the austere regime of Mao. The food of France,
although it has gone off disastrously, is still the
best there is. But we are headed for a gastronomic
Dark Time, such as followed the breakup of class-
ical civilization, and nobody younger than Root
and I are can remember the twilight.

My lamented mentor, Mirande, could remember the full glow of the sun, before the First
World War. "After the First War, everything had
already changed," Mirande wrote in 1952, when
he was seventy-seven. "The mentality of today began to show the tip of its ear." One thing that
changed early was the position of the women he
called *les courtisanes de marque*—the famous
women of the town—and this had a prodigious, if
indirect, effect upon the sumptuary arts. "Yes,
Paris was radiant, elegant, and refined," Mirande
wrote of his heaven before 1914. "In the world
and in the half-world, feasts followed upon feasts,

wild nights upon vertiginous suppers. It was the courtesans' *grande époque*. Innocent of preoccupation with the future, they had no trace of a desire to build up an income for old age. They were gamblers, beautiful gamblers, with a certain natural distinction in their ways and a *je ne sais quoi* of good breeding—the bonnet thrown over the windmill, but without falling into vulgarity or coarseness. They had a tone—a tone as distinct from the society woman's as from the fancy girl's. All the successful demimondaines ordered their clothes from the great couturiers. Their carriages were splendid, better turned out for a drive in the Bois than those of duchesses and ambassadors." Moreover, these town toasts ate magnificently, and boasted of the quality of the meals their admirers provided for them. It was the age not only of the dazzling public supper but of the *cabinet particulier*, where even a bourgeois seduction was preceded by an eleven-course meal. With these altruistic sensualists, a menu of superior imagination could prove more effective than a gift of Suez shares; besides, the ladies' hosts had the pleasure of sharing the meals they had to pay for. The *courtisanes de marque* were substantial in a Venus de Milo-y, just short of billowy way. Waists and ankles tapered, but their owners provided a lot for them to taper from. Eating was a *soin de beauté* that the girls enjoyed.

The successful Frenchman of the early nineteen-hundreds was fat; it was the evidence of his success, an economic caste mark. To be thin at thirty was a handicap in the world of affairs, the equivalent in our culture of driving a year-before-last automobile. It indicated that one had never been in a position to eat one's fill. Caricature accents but does not reverse reality, and I cherish a special twenty-four-page number of *L'Assiette au Beurre,* a journal of savage caricature, printed in 1902 and devoted to "*Le Singe,*" which was, and is, argot for "the employer." Every successful *singe* in the issue —rapacious, lecherous, murderous—is fat. The only unfat *singe* is the one on the last page—an obviously unsuccessful pimp who is beating up a thin girl, clearly not a *courtisane de marque.*

By 1927, however, the celebrated belles, amateur and professional, had become even more skeletal than they are today. Lady Diana Manners and Rosamond Pinchot, the international beauties paired in Max Reinhardt's *The Miracle,* for example, were as leggy and flat as a pair of handsome young giraffes. It was no longer any use taking a woman to a great restaurant except to show her off. She would not eat, and, out of ill temper disguised as solicitude for her escort's health, she would put him off his feed as well. The chic restaurants of Paris—which were none of my or Root's concern at the moment—were already beginning their transition from shrines of *dégustation* to showcases for the flapper figure. The men, too, had turned to the mortification of the flesh, though less drastically. Without exception, the chaps who emerged from the trenches at the end of the war had lost weight, and at such a time everyone wants to resemble a hero.

Of the victorious commanders, only Joffre and

Sarrail had figures like Napoleon's, and they had not been conspicuously successful. Foch and Pétain were ramrods, like Pershing. Also, *le sport*, which before the war had been considered a form of eccentricity, was now taken seriously. When Lacoste, Cochet, and Borotra beat the United States for the Davis Cup that very spring, the sensation was greater than when Lindbergh completed his transatlantic flight. There was also a wave of that endemic European malady *americo-mimesis;* the attack in the twenties is often forgotten by contemporary Europeans in their rage against the bigger one now in progress. The infection then was carried by jazz and by American silent moving pictures, which had nearly wiped out European films. (The injection of the human voice into movies and the resultant language barrier gave the foreign cinema a reprieve that became permanent.) And, finally, there was the legend of the Perpetual Boom. America, it appeared, was the country that had discovered an infallible system for beating the races. This made Americans, in the abstract, as unpopular as we eventually became in the forties, but it also spurred imitative identification. The silent-film comedian Harold Lloyd, who played go-getting young businessman types, energetic to the point of acrobacy, was the pattern-symbol of the Frenchman disgusted with old methods. Even a dilettante can still spot Frenchmen of that vintage by their tortoise-shell glasses and their briskness. (Jacques Soustelle is a classic specimen.) Their costume has become fixed, like the Sikh's turban. The crash of 1929 discredited the original motivation of the mimesis, but the Frenchman trapped by habit behind his tortoise-shells had forgotten why he put them on.

In 1927, these changes were beginning to be reflected in the composition of the restaurant world. The 1925 edition of the *Guide du Gourmand à Paris* listed six restaurants as its *"peloton de tête,"* or leading platoon: Montagné, Larue, Foyot, Voisin, Paillard, and La Tour d'Argent, all "temples of gastronomy" for serious feeders. (Of the first five, all venerable, four ceased to exist even before the declaration of the Second World War. Larue maintained its majestic style through the winter of the *drôle de guerre*, 1939-40, but has disappeared since, to be replaced by an establishment called Queenie's, whose name, as the French say, is a program. La Tour d'Argent, in order to continue, has gone in heavily for public relations, and floodlights itself at night, like a national monument. Such expedients may be justified as being necessary to survival, but they cast a shadow on the age that renders them necessary.)

The specialties that the *Guide* listed as the glories of these great houses in their declining years were not of a sort to accord with low-calorie diets or with the new cult of the human liver. Before the First World War, the doctors of France had been a submissive and well-mannered breed, who recognized that their role was to facilitate gluttony, not discourage it. They returned to civilian life full of a new sense of authority, gained from the habit of amputation. Instead of continuing, as in the past, to alleviate indigestion, assuage dyspepsia, and solace attacks of gout, they proposed the amputation of three or four courses from their patients' habitual repasts. Since the innovators were, as always, the doctors most in fashion, the first patients to be affected were the most fashionable—precisely those who patronized the most expensive restaurants. The *Guide* listed Montagné's greatest attractions as "meats and fish under a crust of pastry; salmon, turbot, prepared *à l'ancienne*, in a sheath of dough; venerable Louis-Philippe brandy. And the coffee! ! !" (The Montagné was the same who edited the great "Larousse Gastronomique.") This is a catalogue of horrors for a man worried about his weight and works, but it was a program of delight for an eater of Mirande's *grande époque*.

The constant diminution of the public that was interested in flamboyant food ended the economic justification of the restaurants staffed to supply it; the new doctrines had the same effect on temples of gastronomy that the Reformation had on the demand for *style-flamboyant* cathedrals. At first, the disappearance of the expensive restaurants was not felt at the lower levels where Root and I reveled, but it slowly became evident, as the disappearance of the great opera houses would become evident in the standards of professional singing; with no Metropolitan to aspire to, the child soprano of Boulder, Colorado, would have no incentive to work on her scales. As a career for the artistically ambitious, cooking became less attractive just at the moment when alternative means of earning a living grew more numerous for the offspring of the proletariat. Child-labor laws and compulsory education were additional obstacles in the way of the early apprenticeship that forms great cooks.

One of the last of the Fratellini family of clowns, an old man, made a television address in Paris a few years ago in which he blamed the same conjunction of circumstances for the dearth of good young circus clowns. "When I was a child, my father, bless him, broke my legs, so that I would walk comically, as a clown should," the old man said. (I approximate his remarks from memory.) "Now there are people who would take a poor view of that sort of thing."

In another area of the arts, Rocky Marciano's preceptor, Charlie Goldman, a septuagenarian, says that there will never again be great boxers, because such must begin their professional careers before the age of puberty, while they can keep their minds on their business. (Marciano, who began late, was a fighter, not a boxer, and fighting is more a knack than an art.) When Persian carpets were at their best, weavers began at the age of four and were master workmen at eleven.

During the twenties and thirties, the proportion of French restaurants that called themselves *auberges* and *relais* increased, keeping pace with the motorization of the French gullet. They depended for their subsistence on Sunday and holiday drivers, who might never come over the road again, and the *Guide Michelin*, the organ of a manufacturer of automobile tires, ominously began to be the arbiter of where to dine—a depressing example of the subordination of art to business. By 1939, the shiny new "medieval" joints along the equally new highways had begun to supplant the old hotels, across the road from the railroad stations, that in the first quarter of the century had been the centers of good, solid provincial eating.

The hotel proprietors' living depended on the patronage of traveling salesmen, whose robust appetites and experienced palates had combined with their economical natures to maintain the standards of honest catering. But the drummers no longer moved by train, doing one large town or small city a day and staying overnight at the Hôtel du Commerce or the Lion d'Or. They were now motorized, and scooted about the highways in minute Citroëns and Arondes, managing to get home to their bases in the larger provincial cities at the day's end. They lunched in a hurry—"like Americans"—and the rural hotels began to die. When the peasants, too, started to become motorized, the small towns themselves began to die. The small-town and small-city merchants had pushed a bill through the Chamber of Deputies prohibiting the great retail chains, like Monoprix, from opening stores in cities of less than ten thousand population, and one result was to accelerate the desertion of the small towns by shoppers; to get the variety and lower prices of the chain stores, they passed up the old centers altogether.

By 1939, the country coyness of the *auberges* and *relais*, with their pastiche medieval décors and their menus edited with fake-archaic whimsey—

the equivalent of "ye" and "shoppe"—had even invaded the capital. "*Humectez vos gousiers avec les bons vins du noble pays du patron en acten-dant les chatouille-gencives du Maistre Queux,*" a Paris restaurant menu was likely to read, in place of the 1926-27 "*Vins en carafe—rouge ou blanc, 50 centimes. Saucissons d'ail, 50 centimes. Sar-dines . . .*" The new baby-talk Rabelais was about as appetizing as, and on a level with, some of our own bill-of-fare prose: "Irrigate the li'l ol' red lane with some of our prime drinkin' whiskey and branch water while the Chef Supreme rustles up an Infra-Red popover Salad Bowl."

The Rue Sainte-Anne is a medium-long street, narrow and totally without distinction, that begins near the Rue de Rivoli end of the Avenue de l'Opéra and runs north toward the Grands Boule-vards; it roughly parallels the Rue de Richelieu, at a remove of a couple of squalid blocks, but it has no Comédie Française to illustrate its begin-ning and no Bibliothèque Nationale to lend dignity to its middle. A block or two before it reaches the Boulevards, it takes the name of the Rue de Gra-mont. It is lined with uninviting hotels, cobbler's shops, neighborhood hairdressers, and establish-ments that sell the drab sundries of wholesale businesses—wooden buttons and hat blocks, pat-terns for dresses, office supplies—and with restau-rants that feed office workers at noon. Among all the restaurants, there is frequently a good one, but it never lasts long. The Rue Sainte-Anne is the kind of street that seems to attract independent spirits. A talented cook who opens there is an Expressionist; he feels no need of a public. There Maillabuau had practiced his art. An American I know once walked in on him between meals to order a dinner for a special celebration. He found the wizard cooking a *choucroute*, or sauerkraut, well *garnie* with *pâté de foie gras*, for three French senators. As my acquaintance watched, he poured in a whole bottle of ancient cognac to improve the flavor. His prices approximated Picasso's.

Yielding to hunger at last, on that evening in 1939 when I walked the Rue Sainte-Anne looking in vain for Maillabuau's, I entered another restaurant, of the same unpromising aspect—a store front muffled in curtains because of the blackout but extruding a finger of light to show that it was open for business. (Everybody in France, at that stage, waged a war of small compromises.) A shabby exterior is no guarantee of good food— perhaps more often it is the contrary—but I was too hungry by then to leave the neighborhood. Nor were the streets hospitable in the dimout. There were no cruising taxis.

Thus it was that I stumbled into the family circle of M. Louis Bouillon, a native of Bourg-en-Bresse, which is the eating-poultry capital of France and in the home province of the great Brillat-Savarin, who was born in Belley. M. Bouillon was a small man with bright, liquid eyes, a long nose, like a woodcock's, and a limp, drooping mustache that looked as if it had been steamed over cook pots until it was permanently of the consistency of spinach. When I entered, he was sitting with his elbows on a table and his head in his hands, contemplating a tumbler of *marc de Bourgogne* as if trying to read the fate of France in an ink pool. Around the table, with newspapers and coffee, were seated Mme. Bouillon; Marie-Louise, the waitress; the Bouillons' daughter, Dominique, a handsome girl of eighteen; and their son, not yet called up for service. (I did not know their individual identities yet, but I soon learned them.) Mme. Bouillon brightened, and Marie-Louise rose and came to meet me. "Sit where you wish, Monsieur," she said. "You have your choice."

There had been a scare at the very beginning of the war, and a great many people had left Paris, expecting it to be bombarded. They had not yet quite decided to come back—it was in the first week of October 1939—and business was, in consequence, dead. I have seldom been so welcome anywhere, or got so quickly acquainted. And I had fallen luckily. M. Bouillon was a great cook. He was not, however, like Maillabuau, a great character actor. His son was in apprenticeship at the Café de Paris, one of the few remaining big classic restaurants. His daughter, that paragon, could make a soufflé Grand Marnier that *stood up on a flat plate*. M. Bouillon told me that he had only recently taken over the restaurant. The rickety cane chairs and oak sideboard looked bad enough to have come from Maillabuau's dispersal sale. But there was food. "The markets are full," M. Bouillon said. "Game, shellfish—everything you can think of. It's customers that lack." I forget what I had at that first meal—a steak *marchand de vin*, or a *civet* of hare, perhaps, before the soufflé, which I ordered to see Dominique do her trick. Then I settled down to drinking with M. Bouillon. He was somber at first. What kind of a war was this, he wanted to know. When would we go out and give them a crack on the snout? In *his* war, the horizon-blue war, the Boche had come as far as the Marne and been stopped within six weeks of the beginning. That put people in the proper cadence. This war set one's nerves on edge. It was the British, he felt sure, who were responsible for the delay; they were perhaps negotiating with Fritz. A war that could not make up its mind had a funereal effect on commerce. The Americans were different from the English, but they weren't in the war. M. Bouillon and I grew sentimental, optimistic, bellicose, and, finally, maudlin. I had a hard time finding my way home, although my hotel, the Louvois, was only a hundred and fifty yards away—a straight line with one turn to the right.

After that, M. Bouillon's restaurant became my advanced field headquarters while I vainly tried to get an *ordre de mission* to go to the front, where nothing was happening anyway. Conditions rapidly simulated normal. The Parisians came back. An ill-founded feeling of satisfaction succeeded the alarm and puzzlement of the first days; the Allies might not be hurting the Nazis, but at least the Nazis weren't hurting the Allies. There was a growing public hunch that the "real" war would never begin. Often, M. Bouillon took me with him on his buying trips to Les Halles, so I could see that

the Germans weren't starving Paris. On these
trips, we would carry a number of baskets, and, as
we filled one after another with oysters, artichokes,
or pheasants, we would leave them at a series of
bars, in each of which we had one or two *Calvas*.
The new Calvados sold at the market bars was
like a stab with a penknife, and at some bars we
would drink Pouilly-Fumé by the glass for a
change of pace. The markets were overflowing; I
recall that there was fruit from Mussolini's Italy
and fine poultry from Prince Paul's Yugoslavia. M.
Bouillon drew my attention to the chickens, which
he said were as handsome as those of Bresse but
inferior in flavor. There was transport, apparently,
for everything but war materials. (I drew the
wrong conclusion, naturally; if there was transport for the superfluous, I inferred, the essential
must already have been taken care of.)

The Bouillon theory was that when we had completed our round of Les Halles, we would circle
back on our course to pick up the baskets, with a
courtesy round at each port of call, and thus avoid
a lot of useless toting. It worked all right when we
could remember the bars where we had left the
various things, but sometimes we couldn't, and on
such occasions M. Bouillon would cry that *restauration* was a cursed *métier,* and that if the government would permit, he would take up his old
Lebel rifle and leave for the front. But they would
have to let him wear horizon blue; he could not
stand the sight of khaki, because it reminded him
of the English.

Of all the dishes that M. Bouillon made for me,

I remember with most affection a *salmis* of wood-cock in Armagnac with which I astounded a French friend—a champagne man—whom I entertained in the little restaurant. I'm sure that it was the best I've had in my life, and M. Bouillon could do almost as well with a partridge, a beef stew, or a blood pudding with mashed potatoes. My Frenchman, as a partner in a good firm of champagne-makers, had to get around to an enormous number of restaurants in a normal year, so when he acknowledged M. Bouillon's greatness, I felt the same gratification that I felt much later when Spink's, of London, authenticated a coin of Hadrian, minted at Gaza, that I had bought from an Arab in Gaza itself. M. Bouillon was my discovery, and the enjoyment of a woodcock signed "Bouillon" was an irreplaceable privilege.

Like most fine cooks, M. Bouillon flew into rages and wept easily; the heat of kitchens perhaps affects cooks' tear ducts as well as their tempers. Whenever we returned to the restaurant from Les Halles minus some item that M. Bouillon had paid for and that Madame had already inscribed on the menu, there would be a scene, but on the whole the Bouillons were a happy family—Madame and the children respected Monsieur as a great artist, though the son and daughter may have thought that he carried temperament a bit far. It was an ideal family unit to assure the future of a small restaurant; unfortunately, the war wiped it out. When the fighting began in earnest, in May 1940, the customers again left Paris. The son was mobilized, and the rest of the family went

away to work in the canteen of a munitions factory. When I re-entered Paris at the Liberation, in
1944, I looked them up and found that they had
returned to the quarter but that they no longer
had the restaurant. To conduct a restaurant suc-
cessfully under the Occupation had called for a
gift of connivance that poor M. Bouillon didn't
have. Since August 1944 I have lost sight of them.

It was in 1939, too, that I was first introduced
to M. Pierre and his establishment on the Place
Gaillon. (The fact that the restaurant is not on the
Rue Sainte-Anne but some two hundred meters
from that street of transition perhaps accounts for
the fact that M. Pierre is still in business.) It is my
favorite middle-sized restaurant; the cuisine has a
robust, classic clarity, like a boxing style based on
the straight left. Everything is done the way it
says in the book, without neologisms or deviations.
The matériel is of the best, the service is deft, and
the prices are rather stiff. M. Pierre has the appearance of a distinguished sinner in a René Clair
movie; in 1939 he had prematurely white hair (to
which his age now entitles him), a high complexion, and an upright backbone. His elegance was
acquired not at the Quai d'Orsay but in the *métier*
in which he made his début, at fourteen. Our first
bond was my discovery that he is a Norman, and
from the proper part of Normandy—he is from
Avranches, across from Mont-Saint-Michel—and,
consequently, an amateur of Calvados, which, to
my taste, is the best alcohol in the world. He sometimes spends weekends calling on peasants in his
automobile and trying to wheedle from them a few

bottles or—wild dream—a small keg of the veritable elixir of Eden. (Every Norman knows that the apple of the Bible is symbolic; it stands for the distilled cider that will turn the head of any woman.) Good Calvados is never sold legally. The tax leaves a taste that the Norman finds intolerable, like the stuff that wives put in whiskey to cure alcoholics. And only a few of Pierre's clients know what they are drinking from his precious bottles; not everybody has had the advantage of a good early soaking in the blessed liquid. Millions of Frenchmen are obtuse enough to prefer cognac, and of late a lot have switched to Scotch.

Even in 1939, Pierre, master of the whole classic repertoire of cooking, admitted that the elaborate numbers in it were no longer in demand. At noon, his restaurant sometimes had the aspect of what Americans were just beginning to call a steak house. "Only twenty-five per cent of my customers order a *plat du jour*," he said to me one day. "The rest take grilled things. It's the doctors, you know. People think only of the liver and the figure. The stomach is forgotten." He tried his best to modify the rigors of this cowboy diet—like a modiste adding a button or a ribbon to soften what the fashion writers call a stark line—by offering superb steak *au poivre*, steak *Diane*, steak *maison* (with a sauce made on a white-wine base), and steak *marchand de vin* (red-wine ditto), but a growing number of customers kept demanding their steak *nature*. "Oysters and a steak, a bit of *langouste* and a mixed grill, a *salade niçoise* and a lamb chop—it's to die of monotony," Pierre said. "If it were not for you and a few like you, I'd drop the *cassoulet* on Tuesday—it's a loser."

The trend has continued since. One evening in 1956, I entered M. Pierre's honest, soothing precincts. The headwaiter—old, gentle, dignified, with the face of a scholarly marquis—led me into the largest room, and in passing I observed a group of six (doubtless three couples) around a table at which a waiter was serving a magnificent *plate côte de bœuf*, while a colleague, following in his wake with the casserole from which the meat had been recovered, ladled onto each plate the leeks, the carrots, the onions, and the broth to which the beef had given its essential tone. The men, I could see, had acquired their jowls, their plump hands, and their globular outlines, uninterrupted by necks —as well as their happy faces—in an age before the doctors had spread the infection of fear; the wives had won their husbands' love, and learned to feel secure in it, before the emergence of the woman with a flat basic figure, on which she simulates a pectoral bulge when Balenciaga's designs call for it, and a caudal swelling when fashion goes into reverse.

When I arrived at my table, I did not even look at the *carte du jour;* my nose was full of the delectable steam of the boiled beef. I said, "For me, a dozen *pleines mers*"—oysters that are a specialty of Pierre's *écailleurs,* the men who stand out in the cold and open them—"and the *plate côte.*"

An expression of sorrow elongated the old-ivory face of the maître d'hôtel. "I am desolated, M. Liebling," he said, "but the boiled beef is not on the menu. It was prepared *sur commande*—the party over there ordered it two days in advance."

That the humble glory of the classic French kitchen should have to be ordered two days in advance in one of the best restaurants in Paris is evidence of how far *la cuisine française* has slipped in the direction of short-order cooking. Beef boiled in its bouillon was the one thing that in the seventeenth and eighteenth centuries, before the development of true restaurants, the traveler was sure of finding at the lowliest inn, where the "eternal pot," drawn upon and replenished but never emptied, bubbled on the low fire that was never allowed to die. "Soup [the *pot-au-feu*] is at the base of the French national diet, and the experience of centuries has inevitably brought it to its perfection," the divine Brillat-Savarin once wrote.

"If there is any left over," the maître d'hôtel told me, looking toward the table of the happy six, "I will be glad to bring it to you. But I strongly doubt there will be."

And now one final instance of lost love on the Rue Sainte-Anne. In June of 1955, I discovered a small establishment there, completely without charm and crowded at noon with employees of neighboring business houses, which posted prices so low that I knew the fare could not be out of the ordinary, though it must have been good value to attract so many people. In the evening, however, when the quarter was quiet and customers few, the proprietor, I learned, could perform marvels. He was a Greek, born in Cairo, who had served his apprenticeship in the kitchens of Shepheard's Hotel and then worked in good restaurants in France before the First World War. Enlisting in the French Army, he had won naturalization, he said, and after the war he had worked in most of the good kitchens that he had not been in earlier. On sampling his work, I gave his story full credence, although it was not apparent to me why he had not risen higher in his profession. His explanation was that he had always been an independent soul—*une forte tête*—and had preferred to launch out for himself. He had mounted small restaurants in Paris, in Le Havre, in Granville— a little bit of everywhere. He liked to be his own boss. An imposing man, he must have measured six feet eight inches from the soles of his shoes to the top of the chef's toque that he always wore— one of the starched kind, shaped like an Orthodox priest's hat. He had a face that a primitive Greek sculptor might have intended for either a satyr or a god—terra-cotta red under an iron-gray thatch. His hands were as big and as strong as a stone-cutter's, and his manner in the kitchen was irascible and commanding. He could be observed in the opening in the top half of the kitchen door, through which he thrust the steaming *plats* when they were ready to serve—and also often thrust his head, toque first, to bellow at the waitress when she did not come quickly to retrieve the evening masterpieces he extended. He would have to duck, naturally, to get the toque through. The round white top would appear in the aperture first, like a circular white cloud, and then, as he moved his neck to the vertical, his face would shine out like the sun—round, radiant, terrible—to transfix the waitress. The girl, bearing the deliciously heavy trays to table, would murmur, to excuse him, "By day, you know, he isn't at all like that. What he cooks for the day customers doesn't excite him—and then it must be said that he hasn't the same quantity of cognac in him, either. The level mounts." The Greek must have been in his middle sixties; his wife, an attractive Frenchwoman some twenty years younger, minded the bar and the cash and the social relations of the establishment; she, too, was fond of brandy. He could produce an astonishing *langouste à l'américaine* and a faultless pilaf to accompany it; I have never known a man who could work with such equal mastery in the two idioms, classic and Levantine.

The pre-eminent feature of any kind of lobster prepared *à l'américaine* is the sauce, which, according to *The Food of France*, contains white wine, cognac, fish bouillon, garlic, tomatoes, a number of herbs, the juices of the lobster itself, and the oil in which the lobster has been cooked before immersion in the liquid. (I have never personally inquired into the mysteries of its fabrication; I am content to love a masterpiece of painting without asking how the artist mixed his colors.) Early in his great work, Root disposes magisterially of the chauvinistic legend, invented by followers of Charles Maurras, that lobster *à l'américaine* should be called *à l'armoricaine* (from "Armorica," the ancient name for Brittany), simply because there are lobsters (*langoustes* as well as *homards*) on the coast of Brittany. "The purists," he says, employing a typically mild designation for these idiots, "do not seem to have been gastronomes, however, or they might have looked at the dish itself, which is obviously not Breton but Provençal, the lobster being cooked in oil and accompanied lavishly with tomatoes—and, indeed, until the middle of the nineteenth century, virtually the same dish was known as *homard à la provençale*. The most reasonable explanation for this name seems to be the one which ascribes it to a now vanished Parisian restaurant called the Américain, which is supposed to have made a specialty of it."

In general, the Bretons practice only one method of preparing their lobsters, true or spiny— boiling them in sea water, which is fine if what you want to taste is lobster. In lobster *à l'américaine*, on the other hand, the sauce, which cannot be produced without the lobster, is the justification of the indignity inflicted on him. If the strength of this dish, then, lies in the sauce (as I deem indisputable), its weakness, from a non-French point of view, lies in the necessity of mopping up the sauce with at least three linear meters of bread. Bread is a good medium for carrying gravy as far as the face, but it is a diluent, not an added magnificence; it stands to the sauce of lobster *à l'américaine* in the same relationship as soda to Scotch. But a good pilaf—each grain of rice developed separately in broth to the size of a pistachio kernel—is a fine thing in its own right. Heaped on the plate and re-

ceiving the sauce *à l'américaine* as the waitress
serves the lobster, the grains drink it up as avidly
as nymphs quenching their thirst. The grains do
not lose form or identity, although they take on a
bit of *rondeur*. Mere rice cooked any old way won't
do the trick; it turns to wallpaperer's paste. The
French in general are almost as bad with rice as
the Chinese, who are the very worst. The Armenians, Greeks, and Turks are the best with it.
The conjunction of my Greek cook's *langouste* and
his pilaf was a cultural milestone, like the wedding of the oyster and the lemon.

At the end of July, six weeks and several dozen
langoustes after making the Greek's acquaintance,
I left Paris. I came back in November, arriving
at the Hôtel Louvois on a chill evening. I left my
bags unopened and hurried through the chill to
the little shrine I had discovered. *Langouste* was
too much to hope for at that season, but the Greek
also made an excellent couscous—a warming
dish on a cold night, because of the fiery sauce you
tip into the broth—and he was sure to have that
on the bill. The aspect of the restaurant had not
changed. There were still paper tablecloths, a zinc
bar, a lettered sign on the window proclaiming
"Grande Spécialité de Couscous." But the faces—
one behind the bar and the other framed in the
kitchen window—were not the same. They were
amiable faces, man and wife, but amiability is no
substitute for genius. I ordered couscous, but it
was a mere cream of wheat with hot sauce and
a garniture of overcooked fowl—a *couscous de
Paris*, not of North Africa, where the Greek had

learned to make his. I had a drink with the new
patron and his wife when I had finished. They
were younger than their predecessors, and said
that they knew and admired them. They would
"maintain the same formula," they promised. But
restaurants don't run by formula. The Greek had
sold out to them, they told me, because he and his
wife had quarreled.

"Why did they quarrel?" I asked.

"Because of their art," the new woman said, and
smiled fondly at her husband, as if to assure him
that nothing so trivial would come between them.*

In 1927, the crepuscular quality of French cooking was not discernible to Root and me, because
the decline was not evident at the levels at which
we ate. The cheap and medium-priced restaurants
that we patronized held good; slimming and other
eccentricities affected only the upper strata, and

---

* One added, final example of the ill luck that haunts *la
restauration contemporaine*. After the tragedy of the Greek
joint, I found another marvel, the name of which I did
not disclose in my *New Yorker* pieces because I wanted
to keep it to myself. It was a restaurant of undistinguished, though not sordid, aspect on the Rue des Petits-
Champs, near the Bourse.

At noon it was *plein à craquer* with *cambistes* and their
employees, which insured its prosperity, but in the evenings serene and almost deserted, which insured admirable service. The *patron*, a real talent, was in his early
thirties, the *patronne*, a doll, in her late twenties. They
were ambitious and acquisitive; the life expectancy of
the restaurant looked, therefore, long. When I returned
in 1960, I had the same experience as in the Rue Sainte-
Anne. The new owners said that my couple had prospered
so that they went in for winter sports. Both had suffered
severe skiing injuries and had had to give up the business! *"Ils sont très handicappés,"* the new *patronne* said.

only the rich had automobiles. Motoring and eating were still separate departments. Root, remaining in France during the dozen years that followed, was perhaps less aware than I of what my lamented Dublin friend Arthur McWeeney would have called the "disimprovement" of French cooking. The experiences of an individual do not follow precisely the descending curve of a culture. A man as wily as Root—gastronomically speaking —might eat so well every day that he would be insensible to the decreasing number of good restaurants. The number was still high then—and is, even now, although, naturally, there are fewer today, and the best aren't as good as the best used to be, or the next-to-best as good as the next-to-best used to be, and so on down the line. Good bottles, however, persist, especially among the classified growths of the Bordelais. The proprietor of a legally delimited vineyard, constrained to produce his wine on the same few acres every year, cannot change his ingredients to fit deteriorating public taste. Good year, bad year, the character of his wine, if not its quality, remains constant, and the ratio of good and bad years is about the same every century. (The quantity of bad wine sold annually in France has certainly increased, but that is another matter; it is sold under labels of vague or purely humorous significance, or *en carafe* as something it isn't.) When the maligned Second Empire delimited and classified the vineyards of Médoc in 1855, it furnished French culture with a factor of stability, such as it furnished Paris when it made a park of the Bois de Boulogne. Both were ramparts against encroachment.* Wine drinking is more subjective than horse racing and nearly as subjective as love, but the gamble is less; you get something for your money no matter what you pick.

So Root the individual was eating voraciously and perceptively, and with total recall, all during that twelve-year interval, and laying the basis for his masterpiece. (I don't think he will ever write a book on the food of Britain. In his monumental treatise, he says, "I used to think . . . that the English cook the way they do because, through sheer technical deficiency, they had not been able to master the art of cooking. I have discovered to my stupefaction that the English cook that way because that is the way they like it.") Root and I, during the *drôle de guerre*, shared some good meals; then for a month, between May 10, when the Germans invaded the Low Countries, and June 11, when the French government quit Paris, we had more pressing preoccupations. (I still remember with gratitude, though, a meal of fresh brook trout and still champagne taken at Saint-Dizier, behind the crumbling front; a good meal in troubled times is always that much salvaged from disaster.) When the government pulled out, Root invited me to accompany him in pursuit of it in a small French automobile. "Maybe we can find some good regional food on the way," he said. I left France for the United States eleven days later; Root, with his French wife of the epoch and

---

* There is a move on to reclassify the growths. I distrust it.

their infant daughter, followed in a month. He returned to France when the war was over, and has
spent most of his time there since. *The Food of
France* is a monument to his affection for a country as well as for its art. He has another French
wife now.

The originality of Root's approach to his subject is based on two propositions. The first is that
regions compel the nature of the foods produced
in them, which is only partly and sketchily true,
and, by extension, that the characters of the
foods, the wines, and the inhabitants of any one
region interact and correspond, which makes for
good anecdote but is pure whimsey. (De Gaulle
has not a poor mind, although his province,
Flanders, has a relatively poor and restricted cuisine; Camus' mind was balanced, not overseasoned
like the food of his native Algeria; Mauriac's is
thin and astringent, not voluptuous like his native
cuisine bordelaise, which he adores.) Root's erudition is superior everywhere but at its best south
of the Loire. Alsace and Normandy haven't his
heart, although he tries to be fair, and he doesn't
perform a sufficient obeisance to Anjou; on Provence, Nice, and the Central Plateau he is superb,
and in his attack on the cooking of the Lyonnais
heroic. Still, to call the cuisine of Alsace an off-
shoot of German cooking, as he does, is as unfair
as it would be to dismiss French culture as an off-
shoot of Roman civilization. A lot has happened
since the shooting in both cases.

In Provence, though, where he has sunned his

well-covered bones during much of the past decade, Root is without peer:

> The grease in which the food of a country is cooked is the ultimate shaper of its whole cuisine. The olive is thus the creator of the cooking of Provence. A local saying points this up. "A fish," it runs, "is an animal that is found alive in water and dead in oil. . . ." Garlic may not belong to Provence alone, but at least it gets special recognition there. It has even been called "the truffle of Provence." A third element must be noted as particularly typical of Provençal cooking—the tomato, which manages to get into almost everything. . . . The rabbits of this area hardly need herbs; having fed all their lives on thyme, they have inbred seasoning. . . . Artichokes . . . are ubiquitous in the region. . . . In the Vaucluse area you may be surprised if you order something listed on the bill of fare as *asperge vauclusienne,* for it is a joking name in the tradition of Scotch woodcock or prairie oysters, and what you will get is not asparagus at all but artichoke. It will be a very festive artichoke, however, stuffed with chopped ham and highly seasoned with a mixture of those herbs that seem to develop particular pungency in the dry, hilly terrain of upper Provence.

This is the lyric portion of the book; it is in Provence that Root's New England heart now lies.

The sounder of Root's two propositions, in my opinion, is his division of all French cooking into three great "domains," in accordance with his dic-

tum that the grease in which food is cooked is the
"ultimate shaper" of the cuisine. Root's "domains"
are that of butter (northeastern and northern
France, the Atlantic coast to below Bordeaux, and
the center as far south as Lyons); that of fat (Lor-
raine, Alsace, and the Central Plateau); and that
of oil (Provence and the County of Nice). The
Basque coast has a mixed cuisine based on all
three media and so refutes the universality of the
system. It is true that the old division of France
by orthodox *fines gueules* into gastronomic "regions" (in many cases smaller than *départements*,
of which there are ninety in Continental France)
has been in the process of breaking down since
the remote date when the abolition of serfdom
made it legitimate for the population to move
around. The Revolution, the diligence, the railroad, and, finally, the automobile ended the pin-
point localization of dishes and recipes—and in
any case, as Root shows, these traditional ascrip-
tions of dishes to places are often apocryphal.

Repeatedly, as he leads the reader about France,
he points out instances where adjoining provinces
dispute the invention of a dish, and where a province that didn't invent a dish does it rather better
than the one that did. There are, however, broad
similarities in the cooking of certain subdivisions
of France that are larger than the old provinces or
the modern *départements*. These similarities (and
differences) do not follow any purely geographic
lines, and Root's "domains" are an ingenious beginning of a new taxonomy; he is like the zoologist
who first began to group species into genera, ob-

serving that while a cat, a monkey, a man, and a tiger are different things, a man is rather more like a monkey than a cat, and a cat rather more like a tiger than a man. Somebody had to start, and Root is a true innovator. Whether the cooking of Périgord really is more like the cooking of Alsace (because both use the fat of the goose and the pig) than like that of the southwest (which, like Périgord, uses garlic) is another question; some future scientist of taste may attempt a new grouping on the basis of seasoning. If the inventor of the new system has as much love for his subject and as much learning as Root, the result can only be another good book, as rich in the marrow of argument as *The Food of France*.

Now that Root's monument has been erected for the ages—a picture of a cultural achievement, fixed to history's page before the snack bars and cafeterias and drive-ins could efface it from men's minds—he seems a trifle melancholy. "It's hard to find such good eating in the provinces nowadays, even at the present high rates—or maybe I'm just getting old and cranky," he wrote me not long ago. "The fact is that it's a long while since I have come upon one of those bottles of wine that make you sit up and take notice, and it's even pretty rare nowadays to have a memorable meal." Here, however, he was unduly somber. There will still be enough good bottles and good meals to last us all a few more decades; it is only that they are becoming harder to find. The rise and fall of an art takes time. The full arc is seldom manifest to a single generation.

VIII

Passable

Following the publication of some of the foregoing papers I had an avalanche of letters—perhaps a half dozen—asking scornfully whether, in my student days in Paris, I did nothing but eat. I tried conscientiously to think of what I did between meals in the years 1926-7, when I was twenty-two–three, and it seems to have been quite a lot. For one thing, in those days young men liked women. We did not fear emasculation. We had never heard of it. This would today be considered a subliterary approach, but there it was. Havelock Ellis was the sage who made authority in the dormitories. Freud had not yet seeped down to the undergraduate level. Molly Bloom was the pin-up girl of the *nouvelle vague*, and we all burned to beat out Blazes Boylan.

Women offered so much fun from the beginning

that further possibilities appeared worth investigating. For this we considered acquaintance, or even marriage, with an undergraduate of the opposite sex insufficient. We assumed, perhaps overoptimistically, that the possibilities of the subject were limitless. They may not be, but no finite man will ever be able to brag that he has exhausted them.

For the beginning student of all essential subjects, the Latin Quarter was an ideal school. The Restaurant des Beaux-Art, as I have indicated, was a great place to learn to eat because the items on the menu were good but simple. The cafés on the Boulevard Saint-Michel offered self-instruction of another kind, but similarly within the grasp of the beginner. You could find any feature of a beauty queen in our cafés, but they were all on different girls. A girl who was beautiful all over would pick a better neighborhood. So, just as at the restaurant, you had to choose a modest but satisfying agenda. In doing that you learned your own tastes.

It was trickier than that because a woman, unlike a *navarin de mouton*, has a mind. A man may say, when he begins to recognize his tastes, "Legs, on a woman, are more important to me than eyes." But he has to think again when he must choose between a witty woman with good eyes and a dull one with trim legs. Give the witty woman a bad temper and the dull one constant good humor and you add to the difficulty of the choice. To multiply the complexity the woman, unlike the *navarin*, reacts to you. She may be what you want, but you may not be what she wants. In such a case she will turn out to be not what you wanted at all.

The unimaginative monogamist has none of these perplexities, but I doubt that he has fun either. I attribute the gloom of many young novelists to an adolescent mistake made at a church. Afterward belated curiosity clashes with entrenched ignorance and produces that *timor mundi* which is the *mal de siècle*. "Ain't It Awful, Mabel?" is their strange device, instead of "Up in Mabel's Room."

The girls would arrive at their customary tables soon after lunch, in late afternoon, and establish themselves with a permanent *consommation*, something inexpensive and not tempting, for they would make it last until somebody treated them to something better. This might be a long time, and they had a skill in husbanding the drink that would have stood them in good stead if they had been airmen downed in the Sahara. When treated, they exhibited another desert talent, the opportunism of the camel. They drank enough to last them to the next oasis.

They spent the afternoon writing on the house stationery. If the waiter caught them doodling or doing ticktacktoes he would cut off their supply. With the hour of the *apéritif* came animation and hope. After the dinner hour, if they had not been invited to eat, there remained animation. It could always happen that, if they kept up their spirits, some late customer would offer them a sandwich. The girls were like country artisans; they took money for their services, but only when they felt like working. On occasion they would accept payment in kind—a dinner or a pair of stockings— but then, as often as not, they would ask you to lend them their current week's room rent.

I suppose some of them had sweet men, but these must have been *dilettanti* too. No protector worthy of the name would have tolerated such irregularity. He would have said the girls of the Boulevard Saint-Michel were not serious. And he would have starved on a percentage of their earnings, like a literary agent who depended on poets. All the girls were young. It was easy to comprehend that this was a phase without a future; there was no chance to accumulate. Where they went after they disappeared from the Quarter I do not know. They were brisk rather than chic, and they made up without exaggeration. My memory is not tenacious in matters of dress, but I am sure the girls wore short skirts—I remember the legs. One girl helped me select a hat for a woman in America, and this would not have been possible except in a period when all hats were essentially alike. It was the age of the face *sous cloche*.

The *cloche* was an enlarged skull cap, jammed down on the head like an ice-cream scoop on a ball of vanilla. For the rest, their clothes were not elaborate, with the short skirt, a short blouse and short jacket, and underneath a *soutien-gorge* and *pantalon*. Having the *points de repère* once well in mind, one saw at a glance what was what.

Sometimes a girl would enter *en menage* with a student, usually a Romanian or an Asiatic. If it was one of the latter, with an allowance from home, the girl would disappear from her customary café for a while or appear there only with him. If it was a Romanian, she would be on the job more regularly than before. Often a girl would make such an arrangement to gain the status of a kept woman, which would protect her from the jurisdiction of the *police des moeurs*.

Once the cops of this unsavory group picked up a girl without visible means of support they would force her to register. Then they would give her a card that subjected her to a set of rules.

"Once a girl has the card she is bound to infract the rules," the girls said. "We are all so lazy. She misses a couple of visits; she is subject to heavy penalties. Then comes blackmail. The police put her to work for chaps who give them a cut. *Hop*, then, no more chattering with student friends who have no money.

"It's the pavement for her, and turn over the receipts to the mackerel at five o'clock in the morning. The police have opened another account."

I was glad to know how things were. It made me feel like an insider, and it helped me understand cops, who run to form everywhere.

Our girls were not intellectuals. None was a geisha primed with poems, nor were there hetaerae who could have disputed on equal terms with Plato, or even with Max Lerner. But all served as advisers on courses of study. They knew the snaps and the tough ones in all faculties, which professors were susceptible to apple polishing and which the most resolutely *vache*. Above all, they had anticipated a theory that was to be imparted to me later as a great original discovery by T. S. Matthews, an editor of *Time*, who told me that the content of communication was unimportant. What did count, Matthews said, was somebody on one end of a wire shouting, "My God, I'm alive!" and somebody on the other end shouting, "My God, I'm alive too!"

It was a poor prescription for journalism, but a good program for conversation between the sexes. (The girls did not keep us at the end of a wire.)

To one I owe a debt the size of a small Latin American republic's in analysts' fees saved and sorrows unsuffered during the next thirty-odd years. Her name was Angèle. She said: *"Tu n'es pas beau, mais t'es passable."* ("You're not handsome, but you're passable.")

I do not remember the specific occasion on which Angèle gave me the good word, but it came during a critical year. I am lucky that she never said, *"T'es merveilleux."* The last is a line a man should be old enough to evaluate.

My brain reeled under the munificence of her compliment. If she had said I was handsome I wouldn't have believed her. If she had called me loathsome I wouldn't have liked it. *Passable* was what I hoped for. *Passable* is the best thing for a man to be.

A handsome man is so generally said by other men to be a fool that in many cases he must himself begin to believe it. The superstition that handsome men are dull is like the prejudice that gray horses quit. Both arose because their subjects were easy to follow with the eye. The career of the late Elmer Davis, a handsome but intelligent man, was made more difficult by his good looks. Favored with a less prepossessing appearance, he would have won earlier acceptance. There are homely fools too, and quitters of all colors.

Women who are both randy and cautious, and therefore of the most profitable acquaintance, avoid handsome lovers because they are conspicuous. He who is *passable* escapes attention. To be *passable* is like a decent suit. It gets you anywhere. *Passable* and *possible* are allied by free association. A young man wants desperately to be considered at least a possibility. But it is the only game in which there is no public form, and he can't present a testimonial from his last employer. He is like a new player in a baseball league where there are no published batting averages. To be *passable* gets him in the ball park without arousing inflated expectations. The ugly man is the object of a special cult among women, but it is relatively small. He runs well only in limited areas, like a Mormon candidate in Utah.

A heartening fact, if you are *passable*, is that there are more *passable* women than any other kind, and that a *passable* man establishes a better rapport with them. Very pretty girls are preferable, of course, but there are never enough to go around. Angèle was *passable* plus—a woman who looks pretty at her best and *passable* at her worst. Her legs, though well-tapered, were a trifle short and her round head a trifle large for good proportion with her torso, in which there was no room for improvement. It was solid Renoir. Her neck was also a bit short and thick—a good point in a prizefighter but not in a swan. She had a clear skin and a sweet breath, and she was well-joined —the kind of girl you could rough up without fear of damage. Angèle had a snub nose, broad at the base, like a seckel pear tilted on its axis.

It was a period when the snub nose enjoyed high popular esteem. The fashions of the day called for a gamine, and a gamine cannot have a classic profile. A retroussé nose, for example, looked better under a cloche. The cloche made a girl with an aquiline nose look like the familiar portrait of Savonarola in his hood. It gave her the profile of that bigot or a spigot.

I had an early belief that I could get along with any woman whose nose turned up. This proved in later life to have been a mistake based on a brief series of coincidences, but when I knew Angèle it still influenced me. Among snub-nosed idols in the United States we had Mary Pickford, Marion Davies, Mae Murray, and Ann Pennington, to name a few I remember. The last two were dancers, and when they kicked, the tips of their noses and their toes were in a straight line. In France they had Madge Lhoty and a girl named Lulu Hegoboru.

Here memory, furtive and irrelevant, interpolates a vision of La Hegoboru taking a refrain of "Tea for Two" in English, in the Paris production of *No, No, Nanette:* "I will back a sugar cack—" as she jumped right, kicked left.

We have no such artists today. The profession of ingenue exists no longer. There was a girl in

Little Mary Sunshine who had the gist of it, but she will have no chance to develop. In her next job she may have to play an agoraphobic Lesbian in love with her claustrophobic brother. The tragic siblings will be compelled to tryst in a revolving door. It is the kind of play people like to write now, because it can be done in one set, in this case the door.

Angèle had large eyes with sable pupils on a pale-blue field, and a wide mouth, and a face wide at the cheekbones. Her hair was a black soup-bowl bob, as if she had put a cloche on and let a girl friend cut around it. (Girls in the United States went to barber shops for their haircuts.) The corners of her mouth were almost always turned up because Angèle was of a steady, rough good humor. Angèle was a Belgian; half the girls in Paris were Belgians then, and all of them said their parents had been shot by the Germans in World War I.

I met Angèle at Gypsy's Bar on the Rue Cujas, a late place outside the circle of tranquil cafés in which I usually killed my evenings. Most of the time I tried to live like a Frenchman, or, rather, like my idealized notion, formed at home, of how a Frenchman lived. The notion included moderation: I would drink only wine and its distillates, cognac, Armagnac and marc. I did not class French beer among alcoholic drinks. In the United States I had been accustomed to drink needle beer, reinforced with alcohol; a six-ounce glass for twenty-five cents hit as hard as a shot of whiskey for half a dollar.

I did not get drunk as long as I followed what I imagined was the French custom. I thought a sedentary binge effeminate. Now and then, though, I would suffer from a recurrent American urge to stand up and tie one on. It was like the *trouvère*'s longing to hear the birds of his own province:

> *The little birds of my country,*
> *They sing to me in Brittany;*
> *The shrill-voiced seagulls' cries among*
> *Mine ears have heard their evensong,*
> *And sweet, it was of thee.*

When this yearning struck during the solvent week of my month—the first after receiving my allowance—I would go to Gypsy's and drink Scotch. The bar was in the Quarter but not used by students. It was too dear. There were even gigolos there—what student would tip a gigolo? I shall not try at this distance in time to guess the nature of Gypsy's sustaining clientele. There may have been a *spécialité de maison*, but I never learned what. I would stand at the bar and think my own thoughts, clear and increasingly grandiose as the level dropped in the bottle. People whose youth did not coincide with the twenties never had our reverence for strong drink. Older men knew liquor before it became the symbol of a sacred cause. Kids who began drinking after 1933 take it as a matter of course.

For us it was a self-righteous pleasure, like killing rabbits with clubs to provide an American

Legion party for poor white children. Drinking, we proved to ourselves our freedom as individuals and flouted Congress. We conformed to a popular type of dissent—dissent from a minority. It was the only period during which a fellow could be smug and slopped concurrently.

Angèle impinged on my consciousness toward the end of one of these reveries. She said that I needed somebody to see me home. In Tours the previous summer, a girl making a similar offer had steered me into the hands of two incompetent muggers. Angèle was of a more honorable character. She came home with me. In the morning, when we had more opportunity to talk, we found that we were almost neighbors. She had a room in the Hôtel des Facultés, where the Rue Racine and the Rue de l'Ecole de Médecine form a point they insert in the Boulevard Saint-Michel. My room, one of the pleasantest of my life, was in the fifth (by French count) floor, front, of the Hôtel Saint-Pierre, 4 Rue de l'Ecole de Médecine, next door to a Chinese restaurant that had dancing. At night, while I read, the music from the dancing would rise to my window and a part of my brain would supply the words to the tune as I tried to maintain interest in the *Manual of Provençal Documents* of Monsieur Maurice Prou. One that recurred often was "*Oh, les fraises et les framboises, le bon vin qu'nous avons bu,*" from *Trois Jeunes Filles Nues*, one of Mirande's great hits.

It was an atmosphere not conducive to the serious study of medieval history, which was my avowed purpose in the Quarter.

Angèle not only lived by day on the same street, but frequented by night the same cafés I did—the Taverne Soufflet, La Source, the Café d'Harcourt, all strung along the Boulevard Saint-Michel. She made her headquarters in the d'Harcourt, where it was the merest chance that she had not re-marked me, she said. She had so many friends, she explained, there was always somebody engaging her attention.

I said that in any case I spent most of my time in the Soufflet, where the boss was a pal of my landlord. But after that I would go to the d'Har-court whenever I wanted to see her. It had a favor-able effect on her standing if I bought her a drink there, and none on mine if I took her to the Souf-flet. If she was not at her post, her waiter would take her messages. He would also tell her to dress warmly in winter and not get her feet wet, to take sufficient nourishment to keep up her strength, and not to be beguiled by clients who had to his experienced eye the aspect of musclemen recruit-ing for a brothel. It was a relationship already familiar to me from New York, where a waiter was the nearest thing to a mother lots of girls had.

When we had established the similarity of our *frequentations*, Angèle and I marveled that we had to go all the way to Gypsy's, a good fifty me-ters from the Boulevard, to find each other. We sounded like the traditional New Yorkers who in-habit the same apartment house but meet for the first time in Majorca.

After that I was with her often. I do not know if she had a heart of gold, but she had what I learned long years later to call a therapeutic personality. She made you feel good.

When I took her out in the evening we sometimes strayed from the Quarter. This was like taking a Manhattan child to the Bronx Zoo. Girls did not shift about in Paris. Clienteles were localized, and so were usages. Montparnasse, although not a long walk away from the Quarter, had all the attributes of a foreign country, including, to a degree, the language.

In Montparnasse the types in the cafés spoke English, American, and German. The girls there had to be at least bilingual. In the Quarter, the languages, besides French, were Vietnamese, Spanish, Czech, Polish and Romanian. But the specimens of all these nationalities spoke French at least passably. The girls consequently could remain resolutely monolingual. The clients were students, or simulated students, at the University. Those were the days of the Little Entente, and France set the cultural and military pattern for the East Europe that is behind the Curtain now. Romanian students came to French universities as freely as if they had done their secondary work in France.

The pre-eminence of the University of Paris was acknowledged as it had been in the Middle Ages. All the tribes rescued from the Austro-Hungarian and Turkish Empires flocked there—Serbs and Croats, Egyptians, Greeks, Armenians, along with Haitians and Koreans, Venezuelans and Argentines. There were also, of course, the North Africans. It would have been a great place to form friendships that would serve in the convulsive years to come. But I thought, if I thought about it at all, that regional convulsions were as out-of-date as *écriture onciale* or horse armor.

Our foreignness made each more confident of his speech than he would have been among the French. From my first appearance in the Quarter, my French was no worse than that of a White Russian or a Czech, and I rose rapidly and successively through the grades of being mistaken for a Hungarian, German Swiss, Alsatian, and Belgian from the Flemish-speaking provinces. Beyond that point I have not since progressed, except in Algeria, where I am mistaken for an old lag of the Foreign Legion who has all kinds of accents so inextricably mixed that it is hopeless to attempt to disassociate them.

Angèle did not like Montparnasse. Neither did I. I had come to France for the same reason that at home I would go out to a beach and swim out just beyond the breakers. There I could loaf. Lying on my back, I would paddle just enough to keep out of the pull, and draw my knees up to my chin and feel good. The Americans in Montparnasse, sitting at their tables in front of Le Sélect and talking at each other, reminded me of monkeys on a raft. They were not in the water at all. One reason I didn't think I liked them was that they had all decided they were writers, or painters, or sculptors, and I didn't know what I was. During my residence in the Hôtel Saint-Pierre I never heard of Gertrude Stein, and although I read *Ulysses*, I would as soon have thought of looking the author up as of calling on the President of the Republic.

Angèle disliked Montparnasse because the people looked at the same time too prosperous and too bizarre. The American women, she said, did not look like Frenchwomen and the Frenchwomen did not look like other Frenchwomen. There were no serious bookstores stacked with doctoral dissertations and tributes to deceased savants. (She herself was not a reader, but she liked academic surroundings.) The types appeared smug and possibly addicted to narcotics. The waiters in the cafés were insolent and Italian, and the *consommations* were overpriced. There were too many fairies and they gave her *drôles* of looks. Let them not fear, she was not in competition. We wound up our tour at the Closerie des Lilas, the border post, at the corner of the Boulevard Montparnasse and our own Boulevard Saint-Michel. The Montparnassiens occupied the post—its tariff was too high for the Quarter. I offered her a whiskey there, but she said it smelled of bedbugs. Now all the French drink Scotch.

Angèle could not get back to the d'Harcourt with sufficient celerity, but once there, it pleased her to have voyaged. She talked as if she were home from a world cruise. But when we went to Montmartre, she was in her glory. She had talked all her life about the *nuits blanches* of Montmartre but had never been there. I took her to Zelli's and we drank several bottles of champagne. She was a solid drinker. All her appetites were robust. In bed she was a kind of utility infielder. She made me buy half a dozen flashlight photographs of us and the bottles, like sportsmen and sailfish, to serve as documentation when she recounted our adventure. Her room, in the prow of a ship-shaped building, was barely wide enough for a single bed. I was there only once, in September of 1927, when she was ill. Half of the mirror was covered with photographs of us at Zelli's.

Aside from her concession that I was passable, which is wrapped around my ego like a bulletproof vest riveted with diamonds, I retain little Angèle said. The one other exception is a report so vivid that I sometimes confuse it with a visual memory.

Angèle told me one morning that she and a number of her colleagues had been playing cards in her room. There were a couple of girls sitting on her bed, a couple more on the bureau, one on the only chair and another on her trunk, when one took off her shoes.

A second girl said, after a moment, "It smells of feet in here!" The shoeless girl said, "Say that once more and you will say *Bon jour* to the concierge."

"You get it?" said Angèle. "The concierge is on the ground floor, we are on the sixth. She will throw her down the stairs. The other comrade who commenced says again, 'It smells of feet.'

"So the other hooks on and drags her out on the landing, and they roll down the stairs together, interscratching with all claws. On the fifth, two law students, interrupted in their studies, pull them apart from each other. The girls couldn't work for three nights afterward.

"One student took up for the girl he had pulled

upon, and the other took up for the adversary. Now the students have quarreled, and the girl whose feet smelled has moved in with one of them at the Facultés, while the other student has moved in with the girl whose nose was delicate. It is romance in flower."

Life in the Quarter was a romance that smelled of feet.

I am afraid that I do not succeed in making Angèle's quality come clear. To attempt a full description of a woman on the basis of a few fragmentary memories is like trying to reconstruct a small, endearing animal from a few bits of bone. Even some of the bits are not much help. My arms try to remember her weight—I should say 118, give or take two pounds.

It makes me wince, now, to recall that she used to butt me in the pit of the belly, quite hard, and that we both thought it chummy. My point of view has changed with the tone of my muscles.

Yet she existed. The proof is that my old landlord, Perès, remembers her well. I sometimes meet Perès at a brasserie called l'Alsace à Paris. The proprietor there is M. Perès' old friend, the former owner of the Taverne Soufflet, which failed in 1931 because he had a wife who did not keep her mind on the business. (It is too much to expect the *patron* of a café to keep his mind on the business himself.) Now M. Robert, whose last name I have not learned in thirty-six years of greeting him, has an excellent wife who does not have to keep her mind on the business. It goes as if on rollers.

M. Perès, who retired from the management of

the Hôtel Saint-Pierre shortly after World War II,
continues to live in the Quarter because, he says, it
keeps him young. He has recently been made an
Officer of the Legion of Honor. He was a Chevalier, *à titre militaire*, as I have said before, when I
first came to live under this roof in 1926, having
distinguished himself by courage in World War I.
I always suspected him of trying to give the impression, however, that he had won the ribbon for
some discovery in Aramaic intransitive verbs or
the functioning of the gall bladder. This would
have been more chic in his neighborhood. During
World War II he served as a captain of infantry,
at fifty-one, and distinguished himself again.

"I was a bit put out," he said to me when I con-
gratulated him on his new rosette, "because my
promotion was slow in arriving. A man of seventy
in the vicinity of the University who has only the
ribbon has the air of a demifailure. But the delay
was occasioned by the nature of my business. The
Chancellery of the Legion is cautious in award-
ing the higher grades to hotelkeepers, because the
hotel may be a *maison de passe*. Once I announced
my retirement, the rosette was not long on the
way."

M. Perès, in thirty years at the Saint-Pierre,
lodged an infinity of students. It makes him think
of himself as a housemaster. "One of our fellows
is raising the question of confidence in the Chamber today," he may say when you meet him,
meaning a Deputy who used to live at the Saint-
Pierre as a student. "He has gone farther than I
would have predicted." Or, "One of our fellows is

now the leading internist in Port-au-Prince—I had a card last week." Or, "One of our chaps who is the professor of medieval history at the University of Jerusalem has, it appears, achieved a remarkable monograph on secular law in the Latin kingdom of Acre. He had your room about ten years after you left. He, at least, worked from one time to another." It is M. Perès' contention that I was a *farceur*, a do-nothing, because we sneaked out so often for a drink at the Soufflet when his wife was in bad humor.

The Anciens de l'Hôtel Saint-Pierre is the sole alumni association of which I would willingly attend a reunion; unhappily it does not exist. If it did, it would include the ladies' auxiliary, *bien entendu;* the girl who lived with the Korean on the floor below me, the mistress of the Dane upstairs, Angèle and subsequent and preceding Angèles of all promotions, and the two little maids from Dax, Lucienne and Antoine, who led the way to the bathroom, which was on the third floor, when the client had ordered a bath. They then allowed themselves to be trapped long enough for an invigorating tussle.

M. Perès remembers Angèle almost as well as if she had made a name for herself as a comparative zoologist in Peru.

She died in the winter of 1927-28, not of a broken heart, but flu. I was no longer in Paris, but in Providence, Rhode Island, where I had returned to a job on the Providence *Journal* and *Evening Bulletin,* and Perès included word of her death, along with other neighborhood news, in a letter that he sent me.

"She had a felicity of expression," he said of her one day thirty years later. "Once she said to me, 'Head of a ruin, how much do you extort for your cubicles?' There wasn't a sou's worth of harm in her. What a pity that she had to die. How well she was built!" he said in final benison.

"She was *passable*," I said.

I could see that M. Perès thought me a trifle callous, but he did not know all that *passable* meant to me.

All Cardinal books in this series are available from good bookshops, or can be ordered from the following address:

Sphere Books
Cash Sales Department
P.O. Box 11
Falmouth
Cornwall, TR10 9EN.

Please send cheque or postal order (no currency), and allow 60p for postage and packing for the first book plus 25p for the second book and 15p for each additional book ordered up to a maximum charge of £1.90 in U.K.

B.F.P.O. customers please allow 60p for the first book, 25p for the second book plus 15p per copy for the next 7 books, thereafter 9p per book.

Overseas customers, including Eire, please allow £1.25 for postage and packing for the first book, 75p for the second book and 28p for each subsequent title ordered.

CARDINAL